CAMPAIGN 332

KULIKOVO 1380

The battle that made Russia

MARK GALEOTTI

ILLUSTRATED BY DARREN TAN
Series Editor Marcus Cowper

OSPREY PUBLISHING
Bloomsbury Publishing Plc

Kemp House, Chawley Park, Cumnor Hill, Oxford OX2 9PH, UK
29 Earlsfort Terrace, Dublin 2, Ireland
1385 Broadway, 5th Floor, New York, NY 10018, USA
Email: info@ospreypublishing.com
www.ospreypublishing.com

OSPREY is a trademark of Osprey Publishing Ltd

First published in Great Britain in 2019

Transferred to digital print on demand in 2023

Print ISBN: 978 1 4728 3121 7
eBook: 978 1 4728 3122 4
ePDF: 978 1 4728 3123 ;
XML: 978 1 4728 3124 8

Maps by www.bounford.com
3D BEVs by Paul Kime
Index by Zoe Ross
Typeset by PDQ Digital Media Solutions, Bungay, UK
Printed and bound in Great Britain by CPI (Group) UK Ltd,
Croydon CR0 4YY

23 24 25 26 27   10 9 8 7 6 5 4 3 2

The Woodland Trust
Osprey Publishing supports the Woodland Trust, the UK's leading
woodland conservation charity.

www.ospreypublishing.com
To find out more about our authors and books visit our website. Here
you will find extracts, author interviews, details of forthcoming events
and the option to sign-up for our newsletter.

Author's note

Translating from Cyrillic texts always poses challenges. I have chosen to
transliterate names as they are pronounced, and have also ignored the
diacritical 'soft' and 'hard' signs found in the original. The only exceptions
are names that have acquired common forms in English – for example,
I use Rus' rather than Rus. I also call what is now known as Kyiv by
the Russianform Kiev to reflect the historical identity of the medieval
cities of the Rus', without in any way challenging modern Ukrainian
preferences. Likewise, Mongol and Tatar words and names are rendered
in the most generally recognizable forms.

Mongol and Mongol-Tatar are also used interchangeably, as makes
sense for the 14th century. There had been an original Mongol tribe
called the Tatars, who had been absorbed into Genghis Khan's imperial
steppe confederation, but when Europeans used the term, they as
likely as not assumed it derived from 'Tartarus', the deepest pit of
Hell in classical mythology. Later, as the Golden Horde disintegrated,
Tatar emerged as the usual term for the descendants of the steppe
conquerors.

Key to military symbols

CONTENTS

The Principalities of the Rus'

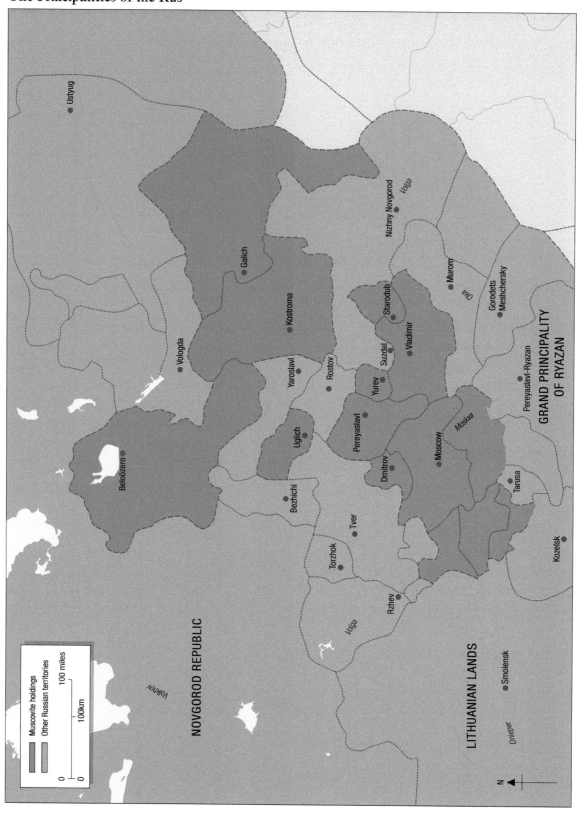

Ustyug

Galich

Kostroma

Vologda

Yaroslavl

Rostov

Uglich

Beloozero

Bezhichi

Torzhok

Tver

Rzhev

Volga

Volkhov

NOVGOROD REPUBLIC

LITHUANIAN LANDS

Smolensk

Dnieper

Kozelsk

Tarusa

Moscow

Moskva

Dmitrov

Pereyaslavl

Yurev

Suzdal

Vladimir

Starodub

Nizhny Novgorod

Volga

Murom

Oka

Gorodets

Meshchersky

Pereyaslavl-Ryazan

GRAND PRINCIPALITY
OF RYAZAN

Muscovite holdings
Other Russian territories

100 miles

100km

0

0

N

ORIGINS OF THE CAMPAIGN

'I want to tell you, brethren, about the battles of the recent war, about how the battle on the Don between Grand Duke Dmitry Ivanovich and all Orthodox Christians and the infidel Mamai and the godless sons of Hagar [Muslims] came about.'

The Tale of the Rout of Mamai

On 8 September 2005, Alexy II, 15th Patriarch of Moscow and all the Rus', and thus primate of the Russian Orthodox Church, declared a jubilee year to commemorate the battle of Kulikovo. Fought against the Mongol-Tatar armies of the Golden Horde exactly 625 years earlier, this was described in the patriarch's address as the battle that 'saved the nations of Europe by shielding them from the threat of foreign invasion.' That might be something of a stretch, given that by this time the Golden Horde was already in decline. It might also appear a strange choice, to honour the 625th anniversary of anything, but the point was to combine these celebrations with those of the 60th anniversary of the end of World War II, another conflict in which the Russians like to feel they saved Europe with their blood and bones. Kulikovo, 1380, and what they call the Great Patriotic War, 1945, are arguably the bookends marking the start and the end – or at least the latest chapter – of Russia's own history as a great, military nation.

The battle of Kulikovo became a powerful symbol of Russian unity and capacity, even if two years later a punitive expedition would see Moscow burned; after all, the legend is often more important than the reality. Dmitry, prince of Moscow, became known as 'Dmitry Donskoy' 'Dmitry of the Don', for his role in this battle, close to that mighty river's banks. More generally, it became part of Moscow's claims to dominate the Rus', and later part of the Russian nation's founding myths, of how it freed itself from foreign domination and emerged as a Eurasian power and Europe's defender alike.

THE MONGOL CONQUEST

'In the same year, for our sins, there came unknown tribes. No one knew who they were, or their origin, faith, or tongue… Only one Russian warrior in ten lived through this battle; in returning to their homelands, many of these were killed by the Cumans for their horses and clothes. In such a way, did God bring confusion upon us, and an endless number of people perished.'

The *Novgorod First Chronicle*

Viktor Vasnetsov's epic representation of the battle was part of a series of paintings of his, celebrating and often mythologizing key events in Russian history. Here the Russians, with Grand Prince Dmitry at the centre, crash into the Mongol lines. Some of the details are inaccurate, including the reliance on fighting on foot and the rectangular, almost Roman shields of the Russians. However, the helmets and armour are reliable, and note the distinctive Russian *berdysh*, broad-bladed poleaxe. (Public domain)

This official picture demonstrates the size of the nuclear missile submarine *Dmitry Donskoy* a powerful asset of the Russian Northern Fleet, photographed here at Severodvinsk. (© Russian ministry of defence)

The deep origins of the battle of Kulikovo lie in the Mongols' conquest of the divided principalities and city states of the Rus' in the 13th century. At this time, the Rus', a mix of indigenous Slavic peoples and the Nordic raiders, settlers and conquerors who had intermarried with them, were characterized by a common culture and disunited politics. Principalities were linked by formal allegiances, family loyalties and practical advantages, but there was no overarching political structure. Indeed, princes would often move from rule of one city to another, seeking to find better berths like modern corporate executives headhunted from company to company. 'Kiev the Golden' was first of the cities, the cradle of Russian Orthodoxy since its forced conversion from paganism under Grand Prince Vladimir the Great in AD 988. Nonetheless, principalities warred for tribute and precedence, squabbled over trade deals, and turned a blind eye to river piracy and banditry waged against their neighbours.

Upon this land of scattered states and cities, divided by deep forests and deeper resentments, came what would become known as the Golden Horde, the western arm of the mighty Mongol Empire. This semi-nomadic confederation would over time ally with and incorporate others, such as the Pechenegs and the Turkic Tatars – hence the near-interchangeability of the terms Mongol, Mongol-Tatar and Tatar in this context – and create an empire that would sweep across Asia, past the Ural Mountains and into Europe. The lands of the Rus' were simply the next objectives as they pursued what they believed was their divine mission of conquest.

The first harbinger was borne by the nomadic Cumans from along the Volga River. Once raiders themselves, they were driven westwards by the Mongol advance, warning the Rus' that 'terrible strangers have taken our country, and tomorrow they will take yours if you do not come and help us.' Concerned at this new and unexpected danger, Princes Mstislav the Bold of Novgorod and Mstislav III of Kiev gathered a force along with their allies from over a dozen

other cities in 1223. Heading east, they met and were roundly defeated by a Mongol army at Kalka River.[1] Nonetheless, what was in fact a mere advance guard of the Horde withdrew, and the Russians told themselves they were safe. They were wrong. In 1236, Batu Khan led a force of some 35,000 cavalry west, crushing the Cumans, Alani and Bulgars before, the next year, moving on into the lands of the Rus'.

The conquest that followed was devastating and decisive. First, Batu turned to the cities of Vladimir and Ryazan. When the latter resisted, it was besieged, its walls smashed with catapults over five days, before the city was stormed, and sacked. Most of the population was killed or driven away, such that, in the words of the *Russian Primary Chronicle*, 'none were left to groan and cry.' Kolomna was burnt, and then Vladimir itself fell, Grand Prince Yuri fleeing while his family died as his kremlin (citadel) burned after a siege in which 'stones fell like rain.' In 1238, flying columns of Mongol troops took and sacked city after city, with siege engines built by Chinese engineers and soldiers drawn from across their empire. Some cities fought bitterly and were defeated, such as Kozelsk, under seven-year-old Prince Vasily. Its defenders held out for seven bitter weeks (in part aided by the way the spring thaw made the land around swampy and inhospitable) before succumbing.[2] Again, the population of the city was killed or enslaved, but Batu was so enraged by this defiance that he forbade any mention of Kozelsk's name in his presence thereafter. Others learned their lessons quickly. The cosmopolitan trading city of Novgorod offered its surrender with alacrity, pre-empting the usual fire and sword with tribute and fine words. Overall, though, the division of the Rus' cities would be their undoing; as the epic poem the *Lay of Igor's*

As Russian history increasingly becomes harnessed to the political interests of the state, the conquest of Russia and its subsequent emergence from the so-called 'Mongol Yoke' has become used to emphasize the importance of unity, strong government, and constant vigilance. This display at the high-tech new *Russia – My History* exhibit in Moscow shows the Mongol invasion under the heading 'Atomization', making it clear that disunity means defencelessness. (© Mark Galeotti)

1   See David Nicolle and Viacheslav Shpakovsky, *Kalka River 1223.*
2   See Konstantin Nossov, *Medievil Russian Fortresses AD 862–1480.*

Campaign put it, 'princes began to argue about trifles, calling them important matters, and created discord among themselves. The infidels from all lands began to invade the Russian land and to win victory.'

By 1240, Batu's Mongol-Tatar forces had driven as far as Kiev. It, too, resisted; it too fell, and suffered the murderous consequences. According to accounts of the time, after it was stormed, only 2,000 of its population of 50,000 survived the siege and subsequent sack. The papal envoy Giovanni Di Piano Carpini, who passed six years later, recounted a city still in ruins, the land around strewn with 'countless skulls and bones of dead men.' Its Byzantine treasures had been taken, its walls broken, and its position as the unrivalled first city of the principalities of the Rus' irreparably damaged.

The Horde continued into Europe, pushing ever westward. It had reached Hungary and Poland before news of the death of the Great Khan, Ögedei, reached Batu. He was called back to join the discussion about a successor, and his seemingly irresistible advance stalled. In 1259, the Mongol Empire effectively fragmented, and a functionally independent khanate formed that stretched from the lands of the Rus' to the west, to the Ural Mountains in the east, and down to the Caucasus mountains and the Black Sea to the south. Only in the 16th century did it acquire its modern name of the Golden Horde; at the time it was called a variety of names: the Ulus of Jochi ('the Realm of Jochi,' after Genghis Khan's eldest son), the Kipchak Khanate (after the particular Turkic nomadic tribe which had dominated the steppes east of the Rus' before being incorporated into the Mongols' empire) or the Altan Ord.

THE RISE OF MOSCOW

'O lark, summer bird, rise to the blue skies on these joyful days of glory, and look at the mighty city of Moscow, sing glory to the Grand Duke Dmitry Ivanovich and his brother, Prince Vladimir Andreyevich!... Their glory is being sung all over the Russian land: in Moscow, horses are neighing, horns are blaring in Kolomna, drums are thundering in Serpukhov, and Russian banners are lining the shore of the mighty river Don.'

The *Zadonshchina*

What the Mongols had taken, though, they would hold. Cities had been laid waste, new dynasties would rise, and, for over a century, the Russians would be under unquestioned foreign rule, trapped in what Karl Marx called with poetic licence 'the bloody swamp of Mongol slavery'. The Golden Horde built a capital for itself at Sarai, on the lower Volga River, to which flowed tribute and princes seeking favours, leniency, and legitimation. After all, the Mongols were conquerors rather than administrators, and they chose to rule through local subject princes rather than engage directly in the tedious business of government.

This provided an historic opportunity for the Ryurikid dynasty, which held Moscow, then just a small trading town recovering from being sacked and burned during the invasion. While other princely families had been decimated for resisting the Mongols, or else had failed to adapt to the new system, the Ryurikids demonstrated that they understood the power of collaboration. Under successive princes, this dynasty proved to be the Mongols' most eager, ruthless and efficient agents, maintaining the hated

This statue clearly shows the typical accoutrements of a high-status Mongol heavy cavalryman. Note the ornate lamellar armour and plumed helmet, as well as the flanged mace, a weapon that often suggested rank. (Creative Commons: A. Omer Karamollaoglu)

census, raising taxes, and crushing dissent in the Great Khan's name. In the process, while doing well for him, they did very well for themselves. Prince Ivan I, for example, gained the nickname *kalita*, 'moneybags', for his wealth, wealth he used buying allies and extending Moscow's influence.

Unlike most dynasties of the time, the Ryurikids came to practise primogeniture, the entire estate passing to the eldest son rather than being divided more broadly into numerous appanages – estates spread around all the sons. This helped concentrate the expanding family fortune. It also

Few could fully grasp the enormity of the Mongols' empire at its height. Those such as the trader-explorer Marco Polo, here shown in an excerpt from the 14th-century Catalan Atlas, were often derided for their accounts of its physical scale and military capabilities. (Public domain)

The Golden Horde

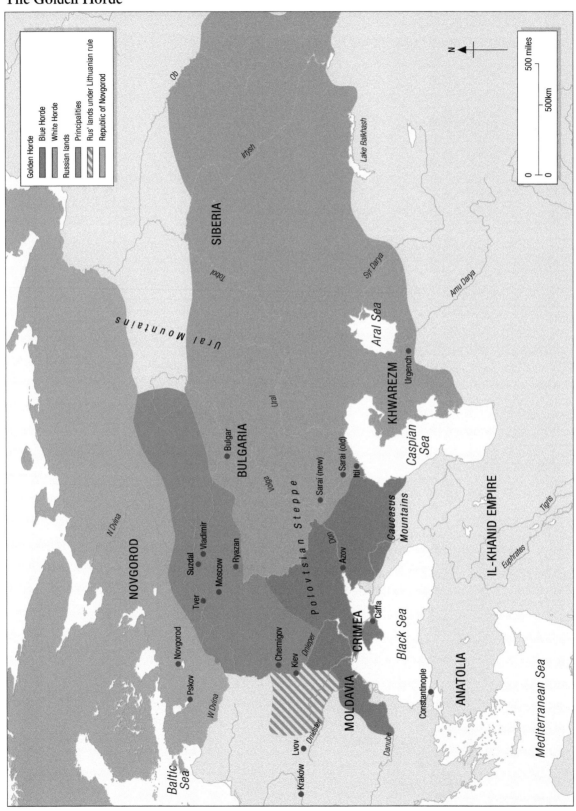

Legend:
- Golden Horde
- Blue Horde
- White Horde
- Russian lands
- Principalities
- Rus' lands under Lithuanian rule
- Republic of Novgorod

N

500 miles
500km
0
0

SIBERIA

Ural Mountains

KHWAREZM

BULGARIA

Polovtsian Steppe

NOVGOROD

MOLDAVIA

CRIMEA

ANATOLIA

IL-KHANID EMPIRE

Ob

Irtysh

Tobol

Syr Darya

Amu Darya

Lake Balkhash

Aral Sea

Caspian Sea

Urgench

Sarai (old)

Itil

Sarai (new)

Volga

Ural

N Dvina

Bulgar

Suzdal

Vladimir

Moscow

Ryazan

Tver

Chernigov

Kiev

Dnieper

Novgorod

Pskov

W Dvina

Lvov

Dniester

Kraków

Danube

Azov

Don

Caucasus Mountains

Caffa

Black Sea

Constantinople

Tigris

Euphrates

Mediterranean Sea

Baltic Sea

allowed for more wealth to be lavished on Moscow itself. Long having been regarded as little more than a tributary of Vladimir, by the early 14th century, Moscow was clearly in the ascendant. Cities such as Mozhaisk and Kolomna fell under its control. Daniil I (ruled 1263–1303) married the sister of Khan Uzbeg and acquired the title also of Grand Duke of Vladimir-Suzdal. In 1237, Ivan I (ruled 1325–40) eagerly led the suppression of Tver when it rose against the Khan, in the process currying favour with his overlords and conveniently enough smashing what was arguably Moscow's main rival of the time.

Moscow acquired new fortresses and monasteries, signs of security and prestige, and in 1327, Metropolitan Pyotr formally moved his residence first from Kiev to Vladimir and thence to Moscow. In effect, it was now the capital of the Russian faith; all it needed to do was assert its claim also to rule the Russian lands.

DMITRY AND MAMAI

> 'There was a weak tsar among [the Tatars] and Prince Mamai was controlling all of their affairs, and he was deeply enraged against the Grand Prince [of Moscow] and all the Russian lands.'
>
> The *Novgorod First Chronicle*

By the middle of the 14th century, the Rus' had recovered from the initial invasion, while the Golden Horde was in decline. The black death, a slowdown in trade along the Great Silk Road to China, bloody and internecine power struggles, and renewed pressure from rivals such as the Grand Duchy of Lithuania meant that the 'Mongol Yoke' was getting looser. Prince Dmitry of Moscow saw in this an unparalleled new opportunity. After all, he needed something to bolster his power. With the Golden Horde distracted, the strength the Muscovites gained from their alliance was reduced. The

Ипонрансивъпелинисинсисоломныисомню
гимнсналмн . нпрншёствна ущисипна
устьблопаснырески ∴

Ипоупрïидеснемоупедникинёгопоеио
Латимо,аенпаснаиёпнуьпмысалцïса
инуишпаснаиёпъ . правпноугïзпе
иïамннпопъсомнwгимнпшннвсипmы
ичпповыинwетаи
памоскпъ ∴

This illuminated manuscript page shows Grand Prince Dmitry and his general Timofei Velyaminov, encamped outside Moscow. (Public domain)

rich and cosmopolitan trading city of Novgorod was already virtually ignoring Dmitry, for example. When, in 1366, the Khan of the Volga Bulgars appealed to Moscow to help stem the depredations of the *ushkuyniki*, Novgorodian river pirates, the Novgorodians responded to Dmitry's appeals that they control the raiders with a mix of defiance and claims of innocence.[3]

In 1359, Khan Berdibek of the Golden Horde was overthrown by his brother, ushering in two decades of chaos in Sarai, as claimants to the throne rose, fell, and competed, often violently. Individual khanates increasingly assumed virtual independence. One such local leader was Emir Mamai of the Jochids, who led the Blue Horde, essentially the western element of Golden Horde. (Confusingly enough, some sources call this the White Horde and vice versa, but here we stick with the Russian usage.) For much of the 1360s and 1370s, he was also a dominant power broker in Sarai, standing as regent behind several brief holders of the throne, until 1378, when the capital was seized by his great rival Tokhtamysh, khan of the White Horde (the Blue Horde's eastern counterpart), and a protégé of the Mongol warlord Tamerlane.

Nonetheless, Mamai was for most of the time in question the decision maker on matters concerning the Rus' and his mishandling of Prince Dmitry can be considered one of the drivers behind his rebellion. In 1362, Dmitry had applied to Mamai for the *yarlyk*, or formal patent, of rule over the city of Vladimir, at the time the most prestigious of the principalities. While his power base was as Prince of Moscow, Dmitry knew that also becoming Grand Prince of Vladimir would bring him glory, honour and, above all, extra revenues.

At first, in 1362, Mamai granted it to him. Then he opted instead to grant it to Dmitry's rival, Prince Mikhail of Tver in 1370, possibly because Moscow was having trouble paying tribute. Dmitry, who already had de facto control of Vladimir, ignored the decision. When Mikhail proved no more able to stabilize the situation – and pay Mamai off – the *yarlyk* was again returned to Dmitry. Ultimately, though, Mamai was himself under

---

3   See Viacheslav Shpakovsky and David Nicolle. *Armies of the Volga Bulgars & Khanate of Kazan*.

pressure and needed generous amounts of tribute to buy influence and force in his struggles for Sarai. Neither Dmitry nor Mikhail could satisfy him, especially as the flow of silver imported from the Baltic Hansa cities began to dry up.

When, in 1375, Mamai yet again transferred the *yarlyk* to Mikhail, Dmitry took matters into his own hands and besieged Tver. Mamai could not help, nor could Mikhail's other ally (and brother-in-law), Grand Duke Olgerd of Lithuania. So he was forced to surrender, and in the subsequent peace treaty ceded Vladimir to his 'elder brother' Dmitry. It was a dramatic development: Russian princes deciding the fate of the symbolically powerful principality of Vladimir themselves rather than waiting to see to whom Sarai would grant it. Some kind of confrontation seemed increasingly inevitable, especially after a Mongol punitive expedition under *tumenbashi* (general) Begich was defeated at the battle of Vozha River in 1378. In the overblown prose of the *Story of the Life and Death of Grand Prince Dmitry Ivanovich*, his forces 'met with the pagan people in the lands of Ryazan, on the Vozha River, and God and the Holy Mother of God helped Dmitry, and the filthy Hagarins [Muslims] were disgraced: some were killed, and others turned to flight; and Dmitry returned with a great victory. And so he defended the Russian land, his patrimony.' Nonetheless, Dmitry knew that all he had done at Vozha was repulse a single raid; it did not change the underlying situation. He was still a vassal of the Golden Horde, and while such victories might give him leverage to secure better deals with Sarai, they also risked triggering even more serious retribution.

Apollinary Vasnetsov's *The Moscow Kremlin in the Era of Dmitry Donskoy* (1922) shows the city before Tokhtamysh's attack in 1382, with the crucial river traffic clearly evident. (Public domain)

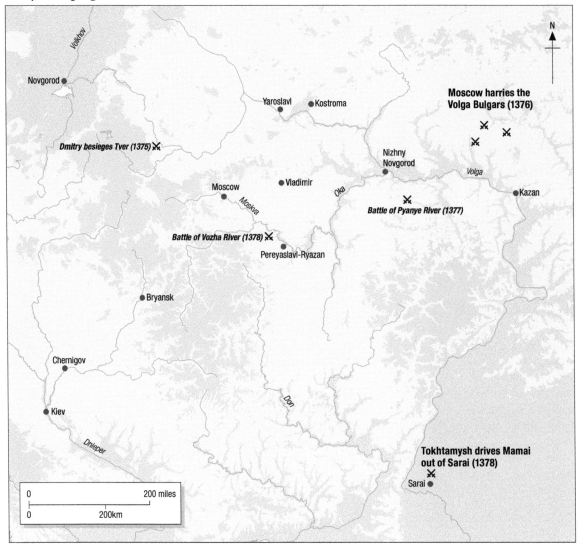

MAMAI'S MOVE

'Grey wolves ran howling from the mouths of the Don and Dnieper, hiding on the river Mecha, ready to rush into the Russian land. But these were not grey wolves but vicious Tatars, who wanted to fight their way through all the lands of the Rus'.'

The *Zadonshchina*

Aware of the Golden Horde's decline and the weakness of Mamai's position, the Muscovite prince felt he was in a position of strength from which to negotiate. After all, much of Dmitry's legitimacy rested on the authority he gained from his relationship with Sarai, just as he knew the Golden Horde depended heavily on Moscow to manage the Rus'. He was not seeking to break the system; rather, he thought this a good opportunity to try and revise the deal slightly in his favour. However, Mamai was thinking of survival,

Once Sarai-Batu, the original capital of the Golden Horde, was a mighty city, the western capital of the continent-spanning Mongol Empire. By the mid-14th century, not least as a result of the civil war within the Horde, it had been succeeded as the effective capital by New Sarai or Sarai Berke, some 180km (110 miles) north-west, and little remains today of its splendours. (© Alexey Dushutin)

not negotiation. He was also now facing a direct challenge to his position from Tokhtamysh, who had just seized Sarai. Mamai needed tribute, which would have to be squeezed out of Moscow. He also needed to demonstrate his power and resolve to the rest of the Golden Horde.

In 1380, then, he sent Dmitry a demand for much more than the usual amount of tribute. Even before this ultimatum could be met, though, he began mustering an army he could lead against Moscow, a force far greater than previous expeditions. Dmitry had hoped to avoid war and was even trying to gather the tribute Mamai demanded, when news of the invasion broke. In the face of this threat, and realizing that the window for negotiation had, for the moment, closed, Dmitry decided it was the time for a bold stroke, a full rebellion against, if not the Golden Horde, at least Mamai. He had, after all, little to lose and everything to gain; his aim was not to liberate the Rus' – frankly, there was little expectation of this and, indeed, no real sense of the 'Mongol Yoke', a term applied only much later, in hindsight – but rather to take advantage of Mamai's weakness to assert Moscow's rise, to use this to consolidate his grip on Russia, and in one stroke to turn a dynasty of quislings into national patriots.

A NOTE ABOUT SOURCES

'I will say this, that the word of God compelled me to write of [Dmitry's] life… I do not add anything from the works of ancient pagan philosophers, but according to his life I give to him truthful praise.'
The *Story of the Life and Death of Grand Prince Dmitry Ivanovich*

It is worth noting that the overwhelming majority of what we know – or think we know – about the battle of Kulikovo comes from Russian chronicles, many of which were written long after the events and by churchmen whose real intent was glorifying the religious dimension of the conflict. Many thus include lengthy accounts of supposed miracles, pious speeches and inspiring homilies, and all too little about the actual course of the battle.

The earliest references come from the *Novgorod First Chronicle*, kept by that city, as well as the so-called *Short Chronicle Tale*, and the *Story of the Life and Death of Grand Prince Dmitry Ivanovich*, followed by the early 15th-century *Story of the Battle with Mamai*. Later that century came the

Expanded Chronicle Tale and a poetic account of the battle, the *Zadonschina* (which roughly translates as 'Beyond the Don River'). By the 16th century, accounts such as *The Tale of the Rout of Mamai* became more detailed, but also layered in a greater degree of religious imagery and miracle. The *Tale of Tokhtamysh* recounts the punitive mission launched against Moscow after Kulikovo. One certainly cannot discount their fundamental details, because they may well have drawn on more contemporaneous accounts that have not survived to this day, but as medieval chroniclers were, alas, less prone to footnotes than modern historians, we cannot be sure. Nonetheless, there is an inevitable degree to which they are based on exaggeration and the formulations of the times. Two other 16th-century accounts, the *Nikon Chronicles* (later developed and re-imagined in the early 18th century by historian and statesman Vasily Tatishchev) and the *Book of Degrees of the Royal Genealogy* were essentially secular, but sought very much to place the battle within the context of the rise of Muscovy. Of course, one can supplement these accounts with everything from archaeological evidence and visual sources to parallels from other conflicts and accounts, but this does mean that there is an inevitable degree of uncertainty, and hence the depressing abundance of 'coulds', 'likelies' and 'probablies' in this book.

There are two relevant Bulgar Tatar sources with direct references to Kulikovo, the *Nariman Tarihi* ('History of Nariman') from the late 14th century, and the 17th-century *Jagfar Tarihi* ('History of Jagfar'), which includes an earlier account taken from the *Book of Bu-Yurgan*. However, these are still essentially outsiders' tales. A particular problem is the relative absence of contemporary Mongol-Tatar sources to balance the Russian mythmaking. The lack reflects many issues, not least the relative unimportance of the battle to them, compared with the struggles of the civil wars then wracking the Golden Horde. However, it certainly creates additional challenges in building up an accurate and even-handed assessment of the conflict.

A surviving copy of the 16th-century illustrated manuscript, *The Tale of the Rout of Mamai*, held in the Moscow State Historical Museum. (© Shakko)

CHRONOLOGY

1359	Dmitry becomes Grand Prince of Moscow on death of Ivan II.
	Murder of Khan Berdibek triggers period of turmoil within Golden Horde.
1362	Dmitry receives *yarlyk* of Vladimir.
1366	Dmitry marries Yevdokia of Nizhny Novgorod, sealing alliance with Prince Dmitry Konstantinovich.
1368	Moscow invades Tver lands: Tver counter-attacks with Lithuanian support and Moscow besieged. Dmitry makes concessions to Tver.
1370	Mamai issues *yarlyk* of Vladimir to Prince Mikhail of Tver.
	Tver-Lithuanian force again attacks Moscow to compel it to give up Vladimir; they again fail to take the city.
1371	Mamai changes his mind and transfers *yarlyk* for Vladimir back to Dmitry.
1375	Mamai returns *yarlyk* of Vladimir to Prince Mikhail.
	Moscow's forces besiege Tver: Mikhail and Dmitry conclude a treaty confirming Dmitry as Grand Prince of Vladimir.
1376	Muscovite forces scour the lands of the Volga Bulgars in response to their raids.
1377	Golden Horde army defeats combined Suzdal-Nizhny Novgorod army at the battle of the Pyanye River.
1378	Tokhtamysh seizes Sarai, driving out Mamai's vassals.

1378	Golden Horde punitive expedition against Moscow defeated at the battle of Vozha River.
1380	
February/March	Moscow receives demand for greater tribute.
June	Mamai begins to assemble his forces.
July/August	Dmitry issues his call to arms.
15 August	Dmitry's forces muster at Kolomna.
26 August	Dmitry and Vladimir Andreyevich join forces.
27 August	Russian forces cross the Oka River.
2 September	Mamai reaches Kulikovo and encamps to await his allies.
6 September	Dmitry's forces arrive at the Don.
8 September	Battle of Kulikovo.
15 September	Dmitry returns to Moscow.
1380/1	Tokhtamysh defeats Mamai at the battle of Kalka River.
1381	Mamai flees to Caffa and is killed.
	Tokhtamysh consolidates his control over the Golden Horde.
1382	Tokhtamysh conducts punitive expedition against the Rus', sacks and burns Moscow and other cities.
	Dmitry swears allegiance to Tokhtamysh.

OPPOSING COMMANDERS

'And [Dmitry] sent for his brother, for Prince Vladimir Andreyevich to go to Borovsk, and he sent messengers to all the princes of the Rus', and to all the governors in the provinces, and to the boyars, and for all the liegemen. And he ordered them to be in Moscow quickly.'

The Tale of the Rout of Mamai

RUS' COMMANDERS

Grand Prince Dmitry Ivanovich of Moscow and Vladimir was undoubtedly the prime mover of his age. His parents, Ivan II and his second wife, Alexandra Vassilievna Velyaminova, died when he was 9, so he assumed the throne as a minor with the churchman Metropolitan Alexei serving as his regent. He struggled under the shadow of his future father-in-law, Dmitry Konstantinovich of Suzdal, known as 'One-Eye', a dominant and overbearing figure, who had ambitions to make the principality of Vladimir his own. They clashed repeatedly, until 1366, when Dmitry married his daughter, Yevdokia (Eudoxia) to seal their alliance. Dmitry followed in his predecessors' footsteps in building Moscow's economic and military strength, not least starting the construction of a stone-walled kremlin – 'fortress' in Russian – that allowed the city to weather several sieges.

Alexei is credited with instilling in Dmitry a strong sense of piety, but also a keen understanding of the political importance of religious authority as political instrument. Ultimately, after all, he fitted the prevailing contemporary stereotype of the Muscovite, a ruthless and self-interested pragmatist. His ruse at Kulikovo, discussed later, of dressing a young retainer in his army as himself, in order to distract the enemy, was arguably as much an act of self-preservation as cunning battlecraft. When Tokhtamysh would later punish the Rus' for the rebellion, leading a punitive expedition that sacked Moscow in 1382, Dmitry first fled the Tatar onslaught and then followed his fellow princes in acknowledging Tokhtamysh's sovereignty. The hagiographic *Story of the Life and Death of Grand Prince Dmitry Ivanovich* may have had it, 'to his friends he was a wall and buttress, to his enemies, sword and fire, cutting down the wicked and burning them like firewood' but he was no sentimentalist; a fierce and energetic warrior on the battlefield, off it he could sometimes be irresolute, but always realistic.

Vladimir Andreyevich of Serpukhov is little known in modern tales, but it is noteworthy that the *Novgorod First Chronicle*, the earliest contemporary account we have, regularly brackets 'Grand Prince Dmitry with his brother Prince Vladimir', suggesting not only recognition of what would prove a pivotal role in the battle, but also a close alliance with Moscow. Serpukhov, 100km (60 miles) south of Moscow, had been founded only in 1339 as a fortified settlement on a steep, riverside hill, to protect the capital's southern flank. No wonder it was entrusted to a close ally, not a brother as the chronicle says, but a cousin, related through Prince Ivan I. He was considered as close as a brother, though, having grown up with Dmitry in Moscow, also being tutored by Metropolitan Alexei. The *Zadonshchina* reports the Grand Prince called him his 'shield of iron in this time of evil'. As prince of Serpukhov, he was one of Dmitry's most trusted commanders, despite having married a daughter of Olgerd of Lithuania. In 1369, at the age of 16, he took part in the defence of Pskov from the crusading knights of the Livonian Order. In 1372, after he had been made prince of Serpukhov, he took the town of Dmitrov, which became part of Moscow's dominions. In the 1375 war with Tver, Prince Vladimir Andreyevich again led armies that were drawn from across Moscow's vassal cities. His reputation was as a personally brave warrior, but also a daring, reliable and inspirational commander, as able in defence as attack, but far more comfortable in the latter. He supervised the construction of Serpukhov's first kremlin, built of oak, but also acquired the nickname 'the Bold' for his martial exploits.

This idealized representation of Prince Dmitry by Sergei Kirillov (2005) nonetheless shows clearly the typical lamellar armour and conical helmet with mail coif of a Russian warrior. His shield would probably have been faced with leather and brightly painted, though. (© Sergei Kirillov)

Dmitry Mikhailovich Bobrok-Volinsky was one of Dmitry Ivanovich's trusted generals, in Russian terms a *voevoda*, voivode, which technically meant a military governor. This was perhaps precisely because he was of Lithuanian or Volhynian stock rather than Russian, coming from a region ravaged by periodic struggles between the Poles, Lithuanians and Rus', and was thus outside the usual web of historical feuds and ambitions of the *boyarin* aristocracy. He was also arguably one of the finest generals of his time. Previously, he had served as a *tysiyatsky*, 'thousander' or militia commander for Novgorod – a position that was appointed on merit rather than bestowed by birth – before taking service with Dmitry at least by 1371. Although he had some administrative duties, his main role was as a Muscovite military commander, leading an army against Ryazan in 1371, harrying the lands of the Volga Bulgars in 1376, playing a part in the Vozha River victory in 1378 and leading the seizure of Bryansk in 1379. He was at once one of the most experienced as well as successful commanders in Grand Duke Dmitry's service, which may well help explain why he was entrusted with a crucial role at Kulikovo, one which depended on calm competence and perfect timing, rather than fiery enthusiasm.

Vladimir Andreyevich of Serpukhov – Vladimir the Bold – is arguably one of the trinity of Russian commanders, along with Dmitry and Bobrok-Volinsky, responsible for the victory at Kulikovo. This idealized image is from his monument in Serpukhov, where he was buried. (Creative Commons: Matavi@)

Andrei and Dmitry Olgerdovich were two brothers of Jogaila of Lithuania. In some chronicles they are described as converts to Orthodox Christianity, but the reasons for their alliance with Moscow were more likely political than religious. Jogaila had just taken power in the bloody succession struggle that took place on the death of Grand Duke Olgerd in 1377. By 1380, Jogaila was ruling in an uneasy partnership with his uncle Kęstutis but Andrius and Dmitrijus – whom the Russians called Andrei and Dmitry – were virtually in rebellion, along with their respective border principalities of Polotsk and Bryansk. Jogaila was both ambitious and ruthless, looking to a dynastic alliance with Poland to create a powerful combined state. There was no room for his brothers in this design. Even though Moscow had taken Bryansk from Dmitry Olgerdovich and instead granted him the smaller principality of Pereslavl-Zalessky, they needed Grand Prince Dmitry's support for both their own safety and in the hope of being able some day to return to Lithuania. If that meant over Jogaila's dead body, then so be it. When they heard of Dmitry's muster they decided, in the words of the *Zadonshchina*, 'Let us mount our fast warhorses, let us, brother, drink the waters of the swift Don from our helmets, and try our steel swords.'

Sergius of Radonezh was neither soldier nor prince, but a monk, and so may seem out of place in this company, but his role in the conflict is emphasized in some later chronicles. Born of minor noble, boyar stock, he joined holy orders when his parents died, and such was his famed piety that he became a magnet for other monks and those who sought the blessings and comforts of the Orthodox faith. His solitary hut near Moscow became the hub for an informal monastery, which in due course would become the Trinity Lavra of Sergiyev Posad. His followers founded more monasteries across Russia, including two in Moscow. Sergius, unlike many of his peers, avoided overtly crossing the line into politics, and turned down an invitation to become the next Metropolitan of the Russian Orthodox Church, remaining the *igumen*, or abbot of his monastery. He was, however, happy to support Dmitry's campaign against what was by then a predominantly Muslim Golden Horde. Later chronicles claim Dmitry sought his counsel before deciding to go to war, to be told 'It is your duty, our Orthodox Lord, to go fast against the pagans and, with God's help, to defeat the godless.' This is likely retrospective myth-making, but Sergius may still publically have blessed him before he set off on his campaign, especially since he had a close relationship with Vladimir Andreyevich. The presence of warrior-monks such as Alexander Peresvet amongst Dmitry's forces symbolized the close alliance, even then, of Moscow's military, political and religious power.

GOLDEN HORDE COMMANDERS

General, governor, and wily politician, **Mamai** was technically not a khan – that title was reserved for direct descendants of Genghis Khan – but an emir. Born in Crimea in 1335, he rose quickly and under Khan Berdibek of the Golden Horde (reigned 1357–59) became first governor of Crimea and the northern coast of the Black Sea, and then his *beqlarbeg* or 'lord of lords'. Mamai's variety of talents were best showcased by this role, as it made him at once Berdibek's master of armies, chief justice and

However inaccurately, St Sergius of Radonezh has been inserted into the canonical Kulikovo story, and this is given physical form with the presence of a church consecrated in his name near the battlefield. (© Alexxx1979)

adviser. When Berdibek's brother Qulpa assassinated him and usurped the throne, Mamai fell from favour but was able in the ensuing years of civil war, treachery and scandal, to manoeuvre a series of contenders into challenges for the throne at Sarai, with him at their back. By the mid-1360s, he was effective ruler of the Golden Horde, his power base being in the Blue Horde of the west, from which he hailed. The result was a growing split within the Golden Horde, with Mamai cultivating relations with Western powers such as Genoa, Venice and Lithuania, and the eastern White Horde falling into more traditionalist ways, culminating in the rise of Tokhtamysh. When Khan Gabdullah died in 1370, many assumed he had been assassinated by Mamai, but nonetheless he made sure he was named regent on behalf of the boy-heir, Bulak, ensuring his own authority.

While a general in name and role, his career demonstrates that he was better in the corridors of power than the fields of battle. Most of the campaigns where he actually led his armies were punitive expeditions in which his forces had a very clear preponderance, and then he was known for the savage and comprehensive way he would loot and burn his way through subject lands. To this day, although the *Story of the Life and Death of Grand Prince Dmitry Ivanovich* claimed that 'the wicked Mamai died unknown', there is still a Russian phrase *kak Mamai proshyol*, 'as if Mamai had come through', to mean something has been turned into a complete mess.

Bulak Khan was born to power, which proved more of a curse than a blessing. The only son of Khan Gabdullah, Bulak was between eight and ten years old when his father died. He was made a ward of Mamai's eldest wife, Tulunbek, and was kept virtually as a prisoner of Mamai, even if in luxurious conditions. When Tokhtamysh seized Sarai in 1372, Bulak fled to – or was moved to – Mamai's power base of Crimea. As power ebbed and flowed, Bulak would several times be re-installed in Sarai, only to have to flee again, but he remained essentially Mamai's prisoner and puppet. He accompanied Mamai to Kulikovo, at an age when his regency ought to be ending, but appears not to have survived the battle. It could be that Mamai made a point of ensuring this, but it is more likely that he was kept in the reserves, but that when they were deployed and ambushed, the young boy-

This portrait of Jogaila by the 18th-century Polish painter Konstanty Aleksandrowicz is idealized, but nonetheless does convey the extent to which Lithuania was already looking west in terms of armour and the overall look; this influence was only strengthened by its union with Poland under his rule in 1386. (Public domain)

who-would-be-khan, eager to prove himself, died in the bloody fighting that ensued.

Grand Duke Jogaila (Jagiello) of Lithuania had only recently succeeded Olgerd (Algirdas), whose son he was by a second marriage. His predecessor had been a ferocious and effective empire builder. Despite the constant threat of incursions by the Catholic crusaders of the Teutonic and Livonian Orders, he had expanded the Grand Duchy of Lithuania deep into the lands of the Rus', stretching through the lands dominated by Kiev to the shores of the Black Sea. His even more ruthless son Jogaila, initially with the support of Olgerd's devoted brother Kęstutis, set himself the task of expanding his authority south into Poland. In due course this would entail abandoning his paganism for Catholicism (he was baptized as Władysław in Kraków in 1386) and marrying Polish Queen Jadwiga, but for the moment he was concerned primarily with concluding treaties with the Orders and securing his own power base. Given that his particular rival, older brother Andrei (Andrius) had found common cause with Dmitry, and given that Moscow's long-term efforts to assert its control over all the Rus' cities would inevitably mean conflict with Lithuania, with its extensive holdings in western Russia, then supporting Mamai was an entirely pragmatic move. The days when Europe feared the Golden Horde were, after all, pretty much over; the days when it might fear a rising Moscow were beginning.

Prince Oleg of Ryazan's decision to throw in his lot with Mamai demonstrates the complex and fluid nature of the politics of the time. Oleg II Ivanovich was personally no more or less content with the 'Mongol Yoke' than any of his peers, but he found himself in an awkward position. Almost 200km (125 miles) south-east of Moscow, Ryazan had not only a history of feuds with its neighbour (especially since 1301, when Moscow had wrenched the prosperous city state of Kolomna from its grasp) but it was often in the front line of raids from the steppe. In 1378, it had again been sacked by the punitive expedition that was then defeated at Vozha River. Moscow was clearly eager to assert its dominance over Ryazan and had repeatedly meddled in local politics, much to Oleg's displeasure. Conversely, if Oleg opposed Mamai, then Ryazan might well bear the brunt of the Golden Horde's responses. As a result, Oleg formally threw in his lot with Mamai, but with the cunning of a born survivor – he ruled Ryazan off and on for fully 52 years – he dragged his feet joining the invading army, while also allowing some of his boyars to join Dmitry's forces, hoping to curry favour with whichever side won. As a chronicler put it, he decided that 'whom the Lord will help, I will support.' Later accounts portray him as the blackest of traitors – the *Expanded Chronicle Tale* calls him 'a sucker of Christian blood, a new Judas' and presents him, through his 'like-minded, Christ-hating' emissary Epifan Korneyev as somehow being an instigator of the whole war – but in reality he was responding to difficult circumstances in a way that would have been comprehensible to his fellow Russian princes, all of whom were used to making compromises with their overlords from the Golden Horde.

OPPOSING FORCES

'This was a force the like of which had not been witnessed amongst Russian grand prices, since the beginning of the world.'

The *Expanded Chronicle Tale*

Many of the chronicles present Kulikovo as an epic clash of huge armies. Over time, the figures given for each side grew: The *Expanded Chronicle Tale*, for example, claims that the Russians mustered 150,000–200,000, while *The Tale of the Rout of Mamai* says 260,000 Russians took on the Golden Horde's 303,000. (Dmitry's scouts apparently reported 'an infinite number of troops are [Mamai's] strength, no one can count them.') It undoubtedly was a very large battle by the standards of the time, but such figures are a ludicrous exaggeration. Even as late as 1500, for example, Moscow's entire population was no more than 100,000. Besides which, Mamai could draw only on the western Blue Horde's lands, and had already suffered serious losses at the battle of Vozha two years earlier. Given that for his 1385 campaign against Tabriz, waged with the full, united resources of the Golden Horde, Tokhtamysh was able to muster a force of at most 90,000 (and probably actually around 50,000), these six-figure claims are clearly implausible. Besides which, the sheer confines of the battlefield – most of the fighting took place over an area of around six square kilometres – itself suggest a sharp upper limit to the forces in play. Instead, a more likely figure was something like Mamai's 30,000–60,000 to Dmitry's 20,000–40,000, which still made this an impressively large clash for the time.

DMITRY'S ARMY OF DETACHMENTS

'Then it was as if eagles were flying from all midnight lands. But they were not eagles flying, but all the Russian princes arriving to help Grand Prince Dmitry Ivanovich.'

The *Zadonshchina*

It was hardly as unanimous as the *Zadonshchina* suggests, but nonetheless, Dmitry's army was indeed like all armies of the age, assembled from a wide range of contingents: princely retinues, local levies, allied war bands and mercenary companies. Dmitry's was perhaps more diverse than many, in itself something of a weakness because of the very variety of types of unit,

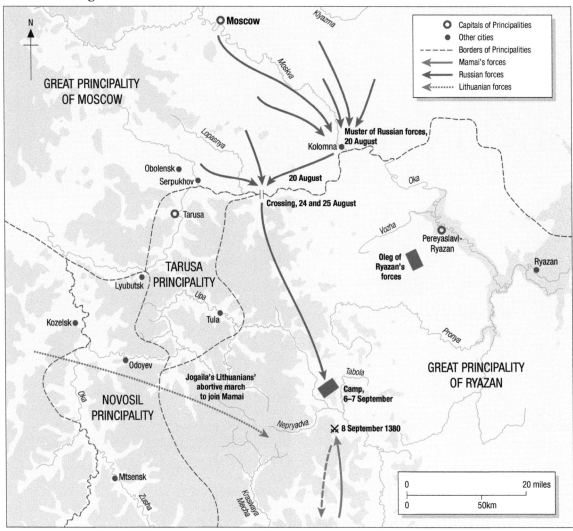

the competing collection of commanders, and even the different languages in play. However, it was also a reflection of Moscow's rising authority, Dmitry's own strengths as a political operator, and a general sense that this was a historic moment that would define the future.

As is discussed below, Dmitry's army was drawn from a wide range of principalities – some, dependants of Moscow, others, which were independent, joining out of fear either of Mamai, or of defying Moscow. Along with Moscow, these included Beloözero, Dmitrov, Galich, Kashira, Kolomna, Kostroma, Mozhaisk, Murom, Novosilsk, Obolensk, Pereyaslavl, Polotsk, Rostov, Serpukhov, Tarusa, Uglich, Vladimir, Yaroslavl, Yelets, Yuriyev-Polsky, and Zvenigorod. About half the total army was composed of forces from Moscow and Muscovite dominions, with the rest being supplied by allied principalities.

Dmitry also had a contingent of several hundred Russians and Lithuanians under the Olgerdoviches. That said, four significant principalities chose not to join Moscow's cause. Ryazan, as already noted, had formally aligned itself

with the Golden Horde, although, according to the *Zadonshchina* chronicle, some 70 boyars from Ryazan were among the fallen on Dmitry's side by the end of the battle. Even allowing for the usual exaggeration, that does imply a reasonable force defying their prince, or being allowed to serve as he turned a blind eye. Prince Mikhail of Tver had been forced to acknowledge Dmitry Ivanovich as 'elder brother' but clearly felt no filial affection or responsibility. Novgorod, the northern trading city, likewise chose not to support Dmitry. Later chronicles, eager to pretend to unity amongst the Rus', claim it was because they heard about his muster too late, but in fact it reflected deep suspicion of Dmitry's chances and ambitions. Again, though, some Novgorodians do seem to have fought at Kulikovo, but probably in a personal capacity. Finally, even if he was Dmitry Ivanovich's father-in-law, Prince Dmitry Konstantinovich of Suzdal and Nizhny Novgorod felt no compulsion to take the field against the Golden Horde.

These detachments were of no fixed strength, ranging from a hundred men to a few thousand at the very high end of the scale. Although they could sometimes be divided, this was often at substantial cost to their morale and effectiveness. Instead, they would typically fight together gathered into larger units known as 'regiments' (the Russian word is *polk*), even if the modern implication of some standard size and organization is wholly anachronistic. Rather, this was close to the 'battle' of Western feudal armies. However, while the European convention was to divide an army into three battles – the vanguard, the middle guard, and the rearguard – the Russians borrowed the five-fold structure used by the Golden Horde, with a Sentry (*storozhevoi*) Regiment, an Advance (*peredovoi*) Regiment, a Main or Large (*bolshoi*) Regiment, and Regiments of the Left and Right Hand (*pravoi ruki* and *levoi ruki*). Although it appears Dmitry may also have retained a reserve at Kulikovo, this is not clear. While that would have been usual practice, it is more likely that he simply detached rear elements from other forces or formed stragglers into an ad hoc regiment on the battlefield, and rushed them where needed.

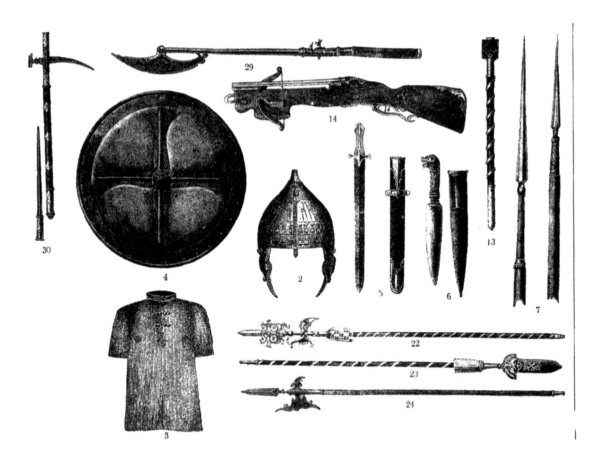

This detail from a 19th-century Russian dictionary shows some of the classic weapons and armour of the time, including the crossbow, the spike-bladed spear, the conical helmet, and the moon-bladed *berdysh* poleaxe. In the last case, what is shown is a later version, incorporating a flintlock gun in the haft. (Public domain)

After all, in so many ways the Russians borrowed their way of war from the Mongols, such that the heart of their armies consisted of fast, hard-striking cavalry formations, as discussed below, recruited largely from the aristocratic boyar class. They were, however, supplemented by a variety of infantry units. These were generally made up of levies drawn from the farms and the towns (including artisans from the *slobody*, untaxed enclaves devoted to their trades), mercenaries, and lesser aristocratic retainers. Footmen would typically wear long shirts of mail or scale and a conical metal helmet (sometimes with a brim round the whole circumference). They would be armed with spears, poleaxes, a battleaxe or sword, or else a composite bow or crossbow. The spear was the most usual personal weapon, generally with a leaf-shaped blade with diamond cross-section, best to penetrate armour, but sometimes a simple boar spear. As well as being a weapon that was easy to find, the cross bar at the bottom of the head of the boar spear, intended to prevent an enraged boar from running down the spear, also could be used to hook a rider from the saddle.

Javelins and darts were still sometimes used, but rarely as a primary weapon. The very first firearms were just beginning to appear in Russia, including the crude handgun known as a *tyufyak*, but there is no evidence of their use at Kulikovo. Crossbowmen would have either a kite-shaped or large pavise shield, while footmen often carried round or kite-shaped ones, typically all brightly painted. Indeed, a Russian army at the time was a colourful affair, as vivid greens, reds and yellows were favoured for shields, clothes and banners.

This picture of a Russian cavalryman, from the 2015 re-enactment of the battle at its original site, shows the classic *barmitsa* ring mail shirt and conical helmet. (© Petr Shelomovskiy)

The quality of the soldiery and their command varied dramatically. The boyars and other cavalry were typically brave and skilled, but also prone to the usual feudal curse of assuming that this was enough, heedless of the tactical needs of the moment. Effective leadership and a capacity to follow orders were, therefore, of crucial concern. *The Tale of the Rout of Mamai* notes that when Grand Prince Dmitry announced a muster at Kolomna, he said that there he would 'reconsider the regiments and assign a commander to each regiment.' This was no passing comment, but a recognition not only that prospective commanders – voivodes – had to be there if they aspired to a position, but also that he was reserving the right to select them as he saw fit. This was already a political gesture, asserting the right of kingship, and, to make it stick, as well as to keep his own grip on this multi-principality force, he relied heavily on his existing liegemen who had been governing cities in his name.

Discipline could also be a problem in other ways. The defeat at Mongol-Tatar hands at Pyanye in 1377, for example, is widely ascribed to the fact that the Russian soldiers got drunk on the eve of battle, while their aristocratic commanders engaged themselves in their own aristocratic pursuits. As *The Tale of the Massacre on the River Pyanye* bluntly puts it: 'if they found honey or beer, they drank without restraint, and they drank drunk, and they ended up drunk. Truly: totally drunk! And their elders, their princes, the senior boyars, the nobles, and the commanders, all of them headed out for the hunt, they behaved as if they were at home.' No wonder the enemy could take them by surprise from their rear, and 'our men did not have time to prepare for the battle and, unable to do anything else, fled to the Pyanye River, and the Tatars pursued and killed them.'

Russian boyar cavalry

'Reliable and experienced in battle, their horses like greyhounds, their armour gilt, their helmets Circassian, their shields from Moscow... their daggers are Fryazhsky [Italian], and their swords Damascene.'

The *Zadonshchina*

Although there is no reason to doubt that Grand Prince Dmitry did indeed take enthusiastic part in the battle, his personal prowess and the injuries he suffered have likely been romantically embellished over time. This 19th-century image by Boris Chorikov of a wounded Donskoy staggering to the shade of a tree is typical. (Public domain)

Although once they had been primarily infantry formations, the heart of Russian armies at the time of Kulikovo was made up of cavalry drawn largely from the boyars – the aristocrats – and their kin, retainers and *druzhina*, or personal guard. In the northern and western cities of the Rus', some had acquired European arms and armour, such as visored bascinet helms and even plate armour for horses, but the boyars largely resisted such imports. In part this had to do with their cost, but to a large extent it reflected the Russians' way of war, which still much more emphasized speed, agility and manoeuvrability, as well as a combination of archery and mêlée, rather than the sledgehammer blow of the knightly charge. After all, it is striking how difficult it often is to tell Russian from Mongol-Tatar cavalry in manuscripts and miniatures of the time. This reflects the fact that the Russians were influenced both by emerging Western European feudal forces and also their Mongol masters.[4]

Indeed, some of Dmitry's soldiers came from the Golden Horde, reflecting the shifting loyalties of the time. One such was Murza Musa, a Tatar who defected to Moscow along with his sons, being baptized and taking the Russian name Pyotr. He was to survive Kulikovo, although all his sons would die, and Prince Dmitry would then marry him into the Ryurikids and grant him a mountainous fiefdom from where his new family name Gora, 'Mountains', would come. His ancestral arms would bear a crescent and star to acknowledge his roots, and a river, representing the Nepriadva River, on whose banks his sons died. Likewise Andrei Serkizov, Dmitry's governor of Pereyaslavl, was the son of a retainer of the Tatar prince Serkiz, who fled the Golden Horde, was baptized, and would acquire lands near Moscow. He died at Kulikovo, but his sons continued in Moscow's service. Dmitry seems to have favoured former Tatars as governors, precisely because their status meant they were outside the boyars' usual networks of family and feud. In fairness, though, this was a two-way process. Similarly, in Mamai's entourage, for example, there was the Muscovite boyar Ivan Velyaminov, who had fled when he fell foul of Prince Dmitry (which turned out not to be a good long-term strategy; most accounts have him captured and beheaded in 1378, although some suggest he fought and died at Kulikovo).

Reconstructions of typical Russian and Golden Horde cavalry suggest considerable commonality in equipment and presumably tactics. Certainly the composite bow wielded by the Russians was a straightforward copy,

4   See Viacheslav Shpakovsky and David Nicolle. *Medieval Russian Armies 1250–1500.*

something noted by travellers of the time. However, that is not to say that the boyar cavalry simply aped the Mongols. As the quote from the *Zadonshchina* that leads this section makes clear, whether or not many of their swords were truly of the legendary Damascus steel, noted for its toughness and tempered edge, nonetheless they were members of a warrior elite from a culture very much at the crossroads of trade east to west, north to south. They had access to ideas and weapons from across their known world.

The boyar cavalrymen of Beloözero, for example, were typical of the elite heavy horse, described as 'strong soldiers dressed in armour, whose horses were in bards'. They would have worn a long shirt of mail weighing anything from five to ten kilos (10–22lb) or, more often, heavier lamellar armour made from small, squared iron plates threaded on straps or braids and worn over padded cloth or leather hauberks. As the rings of mail offered little protection against arrows, the richer warriors preferred lamellar, often adorning them – in a

While most Russian helmets were simpler, lower conical ones, often with a nose guard, they also used this distinctive variation, taller and with a narrow brim. This ornate version, dating back to Dmitry's time, was likely more for show than battle, and is now preserved in the Kremlin. (Creative Commons: Wikipedia/Shakko)

clear borrowing from Mongol-Tatar practice – with a metal disk worn on the chest. This provided both extra protection and also a visible symbol of wealth, as it was generally finely engraved or gilded. Rigid steel greaves and vambraces might be worn to protect the legs and arms, respectively. On their heads, these knights wore a mail coif and a conical helmet, sometimes fitted with a hinged, solid face mask or, more often, a mail veil. As noted above, their horses would also frequently be armoured, with bardings of painted or varnished lamellar armour on quilted pads strapped to the horse's body, along with metal or leather masks.

Even heavy cavalry might sometimes carry a composite bow, in Mongol style. Beyond that, cavalry were typically armed with a lance or spear and a hand weapon, sometimes a mace but more usually a sword, either the heavy sabre favoured by the Mongols or, increasingly, a heavy, long, straight broadsword of Western style with a single cutting edge. They would also carry a shield made of wood, covered in leather or canvas, which was round or kite-shaped, but sometimes a convex trapezoid, similar to the medieval Western *bouche*. In either case, the shield would be brightly painted, and accounts attest to the colourfulness of a Russian army.

THE GOLDEN HORDE

'Let's move, my dark forces and commanders, my princes! Let's go!'
The *Expanded Chronicle Tale*

The details of Mamai's forces are much less clear, given the paucity of records on their side and the unreliability on this point of the Russian chronicle. It

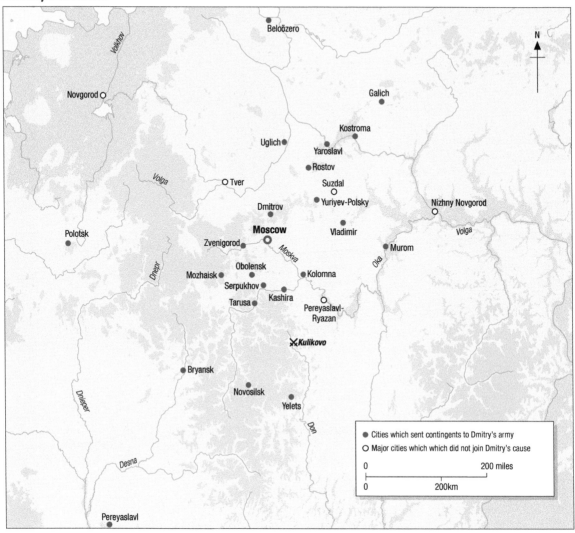

was said that he gathered 'nine hosts and fifty princes', though, and, even allowing for poetic licence, the likelihood is indeed that his army was made up of nine divisions, known as *tumens*. In earlier times, these comprised 10,000 men in a decimal command structure divided into the 1,000-man *mingham*, the 100-man *zuut* (or *jagun*) and the 10-man *aravt* (or *arban*). From the 14th century, though, the Golden Horde's *tumen* had become much less standardized, just as the Mongol-Tatar soldiers, while still formidable, had lost some of the raw edge and nomad toughness which had propelled their ancestors across Eurasia. The *aravt-zuut-minghan* structure remained, broadly analogous to modern squads, companies and regiments, but by then, a *tumen* could be anything from little larger than a *minghan* to the old, 10,000-man complement (and some 40,000 horses, too). After all, as nomads became sedentary, fixed in their lives, a *tumen* might mean 10,000 households, which could not produce anything like 10,000 fighting men without severe economic disruption. Nine *tumens* could thus, in theory, have meant 90,000 troops, but in fact there were likely rather fewer, with each *tumen* probably averaging 3,000 men – this may explain some of the exaggerated numbers that chronicles grant Mamai's army.

According to some accounts, the Tatars from the Volga were unwilling to join with Mamai, because he had failed to protect them from the raids of Novgorodian river pirates. Otherwise he appears to have been able to gather forces widely from the Blue Horde lands under his control. As governor of Crimea, this was his particular power base, and his best heavy cavalry came from the Crimean Tatar tribes, as well as infantry levies from Qirim (now Stary Krym), fortress-capital of the region. Beyond that, though, he drew on other Tatar tribes from Atelkuzu – what are now the southern Ukrainian provinces of Mykolaiv, Kherson, Zaporizhiya, Dnipropetrovsk and Donetsk – as well as allies and vassals from farther afield.

The Golden Horde had inherited Genghis Khan's decimal command structure, with the *arban-u dargas* in charge of *aravts* reporting to the *jagutu-iin dargas* of the *zuuts* and they in turn to the *minghan-u noyan* who led *minghans*. Russian sources talk evocatively of Mamai's 'dark princes' but this was because they used the term *tyemnik*, 'shadowman', for the commander of a *tumen*, a term which actually had nothing to do with shadows in the original, and which in any case was less often used by the Mongol-Tatars themselves than *noyan*. However, given the extensive use of auxiliary and mercenary forces, the overall command structure was more complex, with the Circassian and Dnieper Bulgars there out of personal allegiance to Mamai, Genoese mercenaries because he was their paymaster, and Armenian troops probably somewhere in between the two. As a result, instead of relying on a unitary chain of command, Mamai had to assign a commander to each of the five 'armies' comprising his overall force, which in practice had to be a Mongol-Tatar, even if heading a force primarily composed of other soldiers.

The Mongol seizure of Vladimir in 1328 was a violent sack, well conveyed by this manuscript image, which shows the invaders' distinctive armour and curved swords, as well as their use of ladders to scale the city walls. (Public domain)

The Mongol-Tatar cavalry

> 'The Tatars were very skilful archers. Some of them would stop to fire, while others were trained to fire on the run, others from the horse at full gallop, and could shoot accurately and without a miss to the right and to the left, as well as forward and back.'
>
> The *Tale of Tokhtamysh*

This was primarily a cavalry army, and the core was made up of Mongol-Tatar horsemen, long known as pre-eminent mounted troops. Heavy and lighter cavalry alike might use both bows and close-combat weapons, although the

former were usually more likely to be lancers and the latter archers. Once the ratio of light archers to heavy horse was six to four, but, by the 14th century, the Golden Horde's armies were increasingly favouring the latter over the former. The Mongol-Tatar cavalry in Mamai's force, for example, was more than half made up of heavier lancers. In part, this reflected the way that neighbouring powers (including the Russians) had adopted their approach to horse archery as well as their composite bows, such that old tactics relying on swarming the enemy from a safe distance no longer applied. Instead, in battle they would depend on an initial charge, followed by a series of often quite local attacks, concentrated on potential weak points of the enemy yet also relatively brief. They would then withdraw, regroup, and attack again, and so on. As and when an enemy was broken, then they could deliver terrible carnage harrying and running down those who tried to flee.[5]

Like the Russians, albeit with slightly greater flamboyance, the Mongol-Tatar heavy cavalry wore long coats of elaborate and often intricately-decorated lamellar armour, steel or iron plates laced into rows (sometimes each plate was individually covered with cloth, secured with a metal rivet), over quilted hauberks or heavy, belted coats. The mounts of heavy cavalry were likewise often armoured. Medium cavalry might instead wear the larger-ring mail known as *barmitsa*. In some cases, the lamellar armour was replaced by scale mail in which overlapping plates were attached directly to a cloth or leather shirt, but this was generally more common with troops outfitted from plunder. Their conical helmets quite often incorporated face masks, sometimes showing grotesque demonic features, or 'veils' of chainmail.

The recurved composite bow was their signature weapon, shorter, at less than 90cm (3ft) across when strung, than that which later came to be known as a 'Mongol bow'. Made from laminated horn, wood and sinew, it had exceptional strength, and could fire arrows reportedly for 500m, although in

5   See Stephen Turnbull, *The Mongols*.

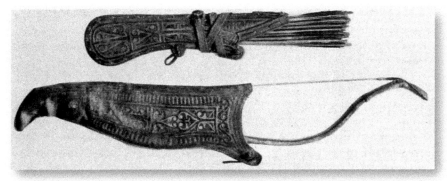

A picture of a traditional Central Asian bow from the British Library collection, in a decorated leather case and with a matching quiver. Many Mongol-Tatar warriors had even more elaborate cases, but the quality of the bow was strikingly standardized. (Public domain)

practice it was more often used at distances of around 100m, at which range it was very accurate and its chisel- or spike-tipped arrows could easily punch through mail and even scale. The maximum effective range was 200–300m. When possible, the cavalry would circle an enemy, showering them with arrows from every direction – what the Russians called the Mongols' 'dance' – but otherwise they would discharge a volley in the charge, holstering their bows in cases on their saddles while on the move, and switching to close-combat weapons.

For that, they typically bore swords – not the scimitars of some representations, but long-bladed sabres – and spears or lances, with narrow heads sometimes incorporating a small backwards-pointing hook to pull an enemy out of the saddle. Maces were also common, with flails less so, with the Bulgar Tatars being the only combatants to use axes in battle with any regularity. Shields were typically round, up to 90cm in diameter, made of leather- or metal-covered wood boards or interconnected rods.

This contemporary manuscript gives a sense of the typical Armenian infantry, with conical helmets, short shirts of chain or scale mail over bright coats, and bearing spears and a halberd. (Public domain)

Mamai's allies and auxiliaries

'That year, the godless, impious pagan Prince Mamai of the Horde collected many troops, and all the Polovtsians and the Tatars, and also hired troops of the Fryazi [Italians] and Cherkazy [Circassians] and Yasy [Alans], and with all of these he went against Grand Prince Dmitry Ivanovich and all the Rus' lands.'

The *Short Chronicle Tale*

As befitted an imperial expedition – as well as one hurriedly recruited from whomever he could find or hire – Mamai's army also included a range of detachments from subject peoples, especially Armenians and Circassians. According to plan, it would also have been supplemented by Oleg of Ryazan's force of perhaps a thousand men, and potentially as many as 5,000 of Grand Duke Jogaila of Lithuania's troops.

The Armenian detachment in Mamai's army was made up of soldiers from their sizeable

Re-enactors playing the part of a Swedish warrior (left) and a Russian (right). Note the typical Russian shield, round with a metal boss, and brightly painted. (© Vitaly Kuzmin)

population in Crimea (they represented at this time the second-largest population on the peninsula, after the Tatars), where they had long enjoyed an enviable reputation as fighters, as well as close relations with the Genoese trading city of Caffa. Mamai may have engaged their services directly as a levy on the community, or potentially hired them as mercenaries through the Genoese, although the former is more likely, given that Crimea was the heart of his power. The force included some heavy cavalry, armoured in *barmitsa*, lamellar and scale, but was mainly made up of several hundred footmen. Some were mailed medium infantry with maces and leaf-bladed spears and round or kite shields, others archers in quilted linen hauberks.

Circassian had become an umbrella term for the Adyghe tribes of the North Caucasus, who had been Christian subjects of the kingdom of Alania until its conquest by the Mongols in the 13th century. Hence the Russians also sometimes called them 'Yasi' from their older name Ās. They supplied horsemen to Mamai's army, as vassals of the Blue Horde. These were largely medium cavalry, famed for their skill and equipped in broadly similar style to the Mongol-Tatars. A mix of horse archers and lancers, their role was to be scouts and also a mobile reserve. They also helped make up for the shortfall in horse archers because of the changing nature of the core Mongol-Tatar horse. Their numbers may have been exaggerated, and were probably at most a thousand (and likely fewer), because Russian sources conflate them with other nomadic horsemen in Mamai's army. According to the Bulgar *Nariman Tarihi* chronicle, for example, there was a contingent of Dnieper Bulgars under one Saban Khalja. These various forces would have looked and fought broadly similarly – especially in the eyes of their enemies.

The Italian trading cities of Genoa and Venice both had important trading stations on the Crimean peninsula to the south of Russia, on the Black Sea. From the Genoese town of Caffa, Mamai had hired a mercenary force of no more than a thousand medium infantry and *balestrieri*, crossbowmen. The former, in the typical style of Italian city militias, bore spears, swords and large shields, and wore mail hauberks and metal bascinets. The *balestrieri* at Kulikovo, by contrast, wore quilted gambesons and padded leather jerkins and bore large pavise shields and daggers. The crossbow was well known throughout the region and although its rate of fire did not match that of the bow, nonetheless its range and capacity to penetrate the armour of the Russian boyar cavalry made it a dangerous weapon. While Genoese mercenary crossbowmen had acquired a formidable reputation across Europe, those to be found in the Crimea were unlikely to be of the same standard (indeed, many may well not have been Italians or other Europeans, but local hires), and they represented probably no more than a quarter of the total Genoese force. Nonetheless, they were serious and effective soldiers, and, given that the Mongol strength was in cavalry rather than infantry, Mamai turned to the Genoese to provide a solid core to his battle line, as well as guards for his headquarters.

Although few Lithuanians actually fought in the battle, and those largely on the Russian side, it is finally worth touching on Jogaila's forces that were marching to join Mamai. He had mustered men from both Lithuania itself and, to a lesser extent, his Russian subject cities. A mix of cavalry and infantry, they would not have looked too different from their Russian counterparts, albeit marching beneath Jogaila's personal banner of a white double cross on a field of red. That said, Lithuanian noble cavalry was increasingly beginning to acquire armour from the West, abandoning conical helmets, with or without brim, for bascinets and even full helms. The infantry was disproportionately made up of crossbowmen, along with spearmen, a mix of heavy footmen in long mail shirts bearing large pavise shields and more lightly-armoured levies, typically protected just by a quilted cloth coat and a metal helmet.

At the battle of the Blue Waters in 1362, Jogaila's Lithuanian forces decisively defeated a Mongol force, consolidating his control over Kiev. This dramatic modern rendition by Artur Orlonov portrays the Mongols as less armoured than they actually were, but shows Lithuanian soldiers of the time, as well as the Mongols' propensity for firing on the retreat. (Creative Commons)

LOGISTICS

'They brought with them flocks of horses, and of camels, and of oxen, of which there was no number.'

The Tale of the Rout of Mamai

Concerned as they were with presenting an exciting tale and praising the right political and religious authorities, it is perhaps no surprise that the chronicles say little about the crucial issue of logistics on both sides. Nonetheless, some aspects are clear, and the relative lack of large settlements close to Kulikovo necessarily meant that both armies had to travel with much of what they required, from portable smithies to repair weapons and armour, to sacks of meal and grains and animals for slaughter.

Dmitry's army had the virtue of being on home territory. Although the modern city of Tula was, at this time, still only a small fortress, nonetheless

Timofei Velyaminov's role as one of Grand Prince Dmitry's trusted commanders is evident in the role he was given in gathering remaining Muscovite troops and bringing them to rendezvous with the main force, here depicted in a 16th-century manuscript. (Public domain)

Kolomna was but two days' hard march away, or six-to-seven days for a wagon or mule train in no particular hurry, within the realms of acceptable resupply. More to the point, a central aspect of his musters in both Moscow and on the banks of the Oka was not just to assemble detachments of soldiers from various vassal and allied cities but also supplies. The general expectation was that a detachment should arrive with at least a week's supplies and enough coin to buy at least two weeks' more, before some units would need to be supplied at another, richer prince's expense (or at least be loaned the necessary funds).

The days when a Mongol army could virtually live off the land were largely gone. Some tribes were still essentially nomadic, still used to living in *yurts*, round felt tents with collapsible wicker frames that could easily be packed away and re-erected. They travelled with days' supplies of millet, cured meat, dried milk curd and kumis (an alcoholic drink of fermented mare's milk). They would also hunt and forage on the move, if need be even drinking the blood of their horses. However, as more and more became settled, they instead turned to agriculture, herding, and more conventional logistics trains, supervised by the officers known as *yurtchis*, who were at once quartermasters and camp commanders.

In this respect, Mamai had two small advantages and a larger disadvantage. Despite his contested claim to dominance over the Golden Horde, he nonetheless did represent its power and could requisition supplies from settlements along the way without necessarily having to turn to force. Secondly, as the initiator of the conflict, he had the most time to prepare his logistical tail. However, he was operating much farther from his real power base in the Crimea, having lost Sarai, which was closer to Kulikovo and thus would have been much more convenient for staging this campaign. His supply lines would also have been vulnerable to raids by local bandits as well as Tokhtamysh's forces, requiring him largely to take and acquire what he needed on the march, rather than count on resupply from the south. This conditioned his rather roundabout route to Kulikovo as he was confined to the west side of the Volga River, and seems to have marched up the right bank of the Don, then crossed it at the mouth of the Voronezh and followed the ridge between the Voronezh and Tsna rivers. This may also help explain his apparent eagerness for battle, as he was counting on being able to take advantage of Dmitry's supplies.

OPPOSING PLANS

'Having gathered all his soldiers, [Dmitry] spoke against the godless Tatars; when they saw the Tatar army was so very numerous, they stopped in doubt, and many were overcome with fear, wondering what to do. And suddenly, at that time, a messenger arrived with a message from the saint, saying: "Do not have doubts, men, respond to their ferocity boldly, without fear, for God will certainly help you."'

The *Life of Sergius of Radonezh*

There is no actual evidence Sergius – later St Sergius – actually sent any such message. As noted above, contemporary and near-contemporary accounts of the battle itself are often sketchy, contradictory, or downright falsifications, hence the continuing debate over the size of the forces and even the precise location of the battle. However, they are especially problematic in terms of the intentions of the commanders. Neither Dmitry nor Mamai's plans were recorded in detail at the time. There are definite exceptions, such as Dmitry's creation of his 'Ambush Regiment', but to a considerable extent we are forced rather to read intent in their disposition of troops and subsequent actions. However, one factor that was clear even to observers at the time, is that ironically enough both commanders felt they needed to bring this battle to a quick conclusion. This would be no game of hide-and-seek, no coy dance of evasion and pursuit; for their own reasons, Dmitry and Mamai were equally determined that this would be fought quickly, decisively, and to the knife.

THE BATTLEFIELD

'Already, brothers, strong winds blew from the sea to the mouths of the Don and the Dnieper, bringing menacing storm clouds to the Russian land, from them springs bloody lightning, and in them, the blue lightning flickers. Thunderclaps peal above the Nepriadva River, between the Don and the Dnieper. Kulikovo field will be covered with corpses, and the Nepriadva will flow with blood!'

The *Zadonshchina*

Both Mamai and Dmitry had also identified Kulikovo Field ('Snipes' Field') in a horseshoe bend on the Don River, 300km (190 miles) south of Moscow as their battlefield of choice. Mamai was encamped along the south of this

MAMAI'S CAMP (PP. 38–39)

On the morning of the battle, before the fog lifts, Mamai **(1)** confers with senior commanders from his chosen vantage point atop Red Hill. Around him, *tug* yak-tail banners flutter in the sluggish early breeze **(2)**. A *noyan* commanding a *tuman* of Mongol heavy cavalry stands beside him impassively **(3)** as Mamai hears a report from the commander of his Crimean Armenian mercenaries, who kneels before him **(4)**. Genoese mercenaries with their distinctive *pavise* shields and polearms stand guard **(5)**, as does a traditional *bankhar* Mongolian sheepdog **(6)**. Mamai's travelling throne is a work of master-craftsmanship, an ivory and wood construction **(7)** that can quickly be dismantled for travel and re-erected wherever he makes his camp. Nonetheless, it had to be left behind and was looted by the Russians when Mamai had ignominiously to flee.

undulating grassland, close to the Gusin ford over the Kurtsa stream to the south, while he awaited his reinforcements. The field offered pasture for horses, firewood from the forests along its edges for warmth and cooking, and the clean waters of the Kurtsa for all. To Dmitry, it provided a battlefield 4km (2½ miles) wide and 8km deep, where Mamai's numbers and cavalry would at least be constrained.

To the north was the Don and its tributary, the Nepriadva, which curved along the western edge of the field, while to the east was another, smaller tributary, the Smolka. This rounded sward between them looked open at first glance, but was broken by small streams and thickets that would interfere with the momentum of a cavalry charge and provide cover for infantry. The thick woods on each side, and steep banks of the Nepriadva also channelled forces in such a way that Dmitry could hope to keep his flanks secure. After all, the fear when fighting such an aggressive and highly mobile army such as the Golden Horde's was always to be outflanked and surrounded.

A shallow ford across the Don, the Tatinki, made deploying from his encampment on the other bank, to the north-east, relatively easy. It is unlikely he did not also consider that in the worst-case scenario it also provided an escape route. That said, the steep, wooded banks of the Nepriadva to the west also meant that if Mamai's forces were able to push the Russian line that way, it could be 'kettled', trapped between them and an unfordable stretch of the Don, with no escape. This very risk, though, also suggested an opportunity for the wily Russian Grand Prince.

DMITRY'S GAMBLE

'Stay here, brothers, in your places, without confusion. Each of you should now make ready, for in the morning it will be impossible to prepare: after all, our guests are already approaching, they are standing on the river at Nepriadva, they are preparing for battle near Kulikovo field, and in the morning we will drink of a common cup with them, as we do in Russia!'
The Tale of the Rout of Mamai

It was just as well for Moscow that Dmitry was both a cunning and a daring commander on the battlefield. He had been aware that Mamai already outnumbered him, even as he was crossing the river Oka, some ten days from the confrontation. But then he heard that a force of Lithuanians under Jogaila was marching to join the enemy, to add to the contingent promised by Ryazan, which would make Mamai's advantage in numbers even more formidable. The news that his enemies were expecting substantial reinforcements decided matters for Grand Prince Dmitry; he needed to win, to win conclusively, and to win quickly.

First of all, he read his battlefield carefully. On learning that Mamai had encamped south of the Don River, near Kulikovo, Dmitry marched his army hard to reach an encampment at Tatinki on the other bank of the river, to the north-east. Detachments of light horse ranged ahead in the hope of avoiding any unpleasant surprises and to intercept any Mongol scouts. In order to minimize the Mongol-Tatar forces' advantage of manoeuvrability, as well as numbers, he wanted to make sure he had the initiative deploying on Kulikovo Field, so that he could maximize its natural, defensive bottleneck.

Although the tale of Peresvet the warrior-monk may be a legend, this modern representation shows clearly the detail of some Russian soldiers and also Dmitry's dark banner. (Original picture © Vladimir Volkov)

Dmitry was the general of his army, but he by no means had free rein. This was an army thrown together from an array of separate detachments unused to working together. Furthermore, this was a feudal army, subject to the usual prickly princely notions of hierarchy and glory. For example, the Regiment of the Right Hand was regarded as a more honourable command than the Left, so princes and knights would resent being assigned to the latter. Given that Dmitry knew the left was where he was vulnerable, this must have complicated his deployments and also helps explain why he preferred to put his faith in the presence of the Ambush Regiment, rather than simply placing more and better troops in the Regiment of the Left Hand from the start.

The Russians moved from their camp early in the morning, under a thick bank of river fog. Not knowing when the concealment of the fog would lift, beyond one specific gambit involving a forest ambush, he moved quickly to lay out his forces in what was a typical arrangement for the times, one all his commanders could easily understand.

In front of the main force was the Sentry Regiment, essentially a thin screen of cavalry and infantry scouts, including some Mongol-Tatars in Muscovite service. The regiment was commanded by Mikhail Ivanovich Akinfov (sometimes referred to as Okinfovich), another of Dmitry's trusted boyars from Moscow. Then would come the Advance Regiment under Mikula Vasilievich Velyaminov, the governor of Kolomna. This also included some of the Lithuanians, a placement dictated by political realities and Lithuanian pride more than battlefield logic. Andrei and Dmitry Olgerdovich demanded the honour precisely because Jogaila was supporting Mamai, and Grand Prince Dmitry could not deny his allies this position. Behind them was the flower of Dmitry's army, several detachments of armoured boyar cavalry and some infantry in the Main Regiment, with his own personal detachment at the centre. The much smaller Regiment of the Left Hand and Regiment of the Right Hand, also of cavalry, would protect his flanks.

The marble relief by Alexander Loganovsky was part of the façade of the Cathedral of Christ the Saviour until it was destroyed on Stalin's orders in 1931. The relief itself was preserved, though, and was later mounted on the Donskoy Monastery in Moscow. It shows Dmitry being blessed by Sergius of Radonezh, and being introduced to Peresvet and Oslabya (on the left). (© Ludvig41)

Then, unusually, there was also a sixth regiment. To a considerable extent, given the terrain and the disparity in numbers, Dmitry could not formulate much of a plan. He would establish the battlefield in conditions of his choosing, but otherwise to a large extent his plan was really just to weather whatever Mamai threw at him, and hope for an opportunity. However, subterfuge would also play a crucial role and allow Dmitry precisely to play on Mamai's assumption that his enemies would adopt the usual battlefield disposition. Taking advantage of both the terrain and the thick fog that blanketed the battlefield in the morning, Dmitry placed a substantial force of some of his best heavy cavalry under his cousin Prince Vladimir Andreyevich of Serpukhov and Dmitry Mikhailovich Bobrok-Volinsky in the woods on his left flank. They were carefully chosen as the most level-headed and reliable of Dmitry's commanders, because they would have to resist the usual, boyar tendency to want to join the fray at the first opportunity. Instead, they would have to wait until the most favourable moment before unleashing the so-called Ambush Regiment. This was a risky stratagem, as it deprived the Russian front line of elite troops it would miss, as well as two of its best generals. However, it would prove to be perhaps the most decisive element of the Muscovite plan, as Mongol numbers would otherwise have won the day. It also reflected Dmitry's accurate assessment of his own vulnerability, rightly predicting that Mamai would seize the chance to push the Russians against the Nepriadva.

Meanwhile, Dmitry also exchanged armour with a young Muscovite aristocrat who would play his role at the front of the army. We do not even know for sure this man's name; it is generally given as Mikhail Brenok, but, given that in the chronicles it is usually in the accusative or genitive form ('Brenka'), some have suggested the alternatives Brenk, Brenko or even, as

This 16th-century Novgorodian horseman would have been immediately recognizable to his forebears, as the equipment and armour were fundamentally the same as worn by Russian cavalry at Kulikovo. (Public domain)

appears in the *Suzdal Chronicles*, Brenkov, but Brenok is most likely. Dmitry was no coward, but he also knew that Mamai would see killing him as crucial both to shattering the Russians' morale and also demonstrating his own might. In these circumstances, the practical Muscovite prince decided discretion was the better part of vainglory.

MAMAI'S HAMMER

'The same wicked king, who will be devoured by the devil himself for perdition, cried out suddenly, beginning "These are my strengths, and if I do not prevail over the Russian princes, how will I return home? I could not bear my disgrace!" And he ordered his godless Polovtsi to prepare for battle.'
The Tale of the Rout of Mamai

However much he was regularly presented as a monstrous figure of evil in the Russian chronicles, Mamai had a formidable reputation as a military commander. It is hard, though, entirely to understand why, given his relatively unimpressive performance on the battlefield, where he shifted between impatience and excessive caution. To an extent, his reputation is likely to have been often not so much because of his own generalship as his having been willing and able to rely in the past on able subordinates. Mamai knew when to trust his fighting officers, and was also a capable operational commander on the political and logistical level, generally able to muster allies and ensure his forces had the provisions and materials they needed. This can, after all, be as important a military skill as tactical acumen.

In any case, this whole expedition was less about Moscow and more about Sarai. The capture of the Golden Horde's capital had also deprived Mamai of some of his usual commanders and a key logistical base. More urgently, his main concern was the threat posed by Tokhtamysh, and his need both to extract more tribute from the Russians and also to prove his own qualities as a khan. Mamai needed a win, but not necessarily a quick one. He was in a good position, and adequately supplied, and there was time before the weather made campaigning hard. So Mamai was not in a great rush to join battle with Dmitry's forces, given that he was expecting to be supplemented by a client army from Ryazan, as well as a force of Jogaila's Lithuanians, even though neither would actually arrive in time to fight (in the case of the Ryazan detachment, quite possibly by design). Having more soldiers than the enemy is good; having many more, even better.

However, once it became clear that Dmitry was eager for battle, and, given that he already had more soldiers, Mamai was certainly not going to retreat. That might allow time for his reinforcements to arrive, but it would also make him look weak. Instead, if need be the detachments from Ryazan and Lithuania could help police up remnants of Dmitry's shattered army

The Norse influence on the Rus' is especially evident in this early 14th-century helmet in the Moscow State Historical Museum collection; apart from the mail veil, a borrowing from the east, this could almost have been worn by a Viking. By Kulikovo, this style would be considered a little dated, but as weapons and armour were often handed down over generations, it would by no means have been out of place (© XIIIfromTOKYO)

after his victory. Besides, he feared a lengthy campaign that would run the risk of being curtailed by the Russian winter. He wanted to be in a position to start focusing and expanding his forces – helped by new silver tribute squeezed from Russia – against Tokhtamysh.

So even if he had not been in any rush to close in the first place, if there was to be a battle, Mamai wanted to win quickly, albeit for different reasons from Dmitry, and he was willing to buy that victory in blood. There was, he would have realized, no point in using such well-loved Mongol tactics as the *mangudai*, starting the battle with a light cavalry attack that would easily be

This picture from the Kulikovo Field museum clearly shows typical scale barding horse armour employed by the Golden Horde's heavy cavalry. (Photo by Stanislav Krasilnikov\ TASS via Getty Images)

repelled, in the hope of drawing the enemy out of their ranks in disorderly pursuit. The Russians had fought against – and alongside – their enemies too long and too often to be so easily fooled. Instead, he thus relied on a relatively simple plan, of throwing successive, closely ranked waves of troops at the Russians to grind them down.

After all, he must have felt that it was a relatively safe bet. He had mustered a force of more than 30,000 men, which was a very sizeable army in the terms of the time, the largest Golden Horde deployment into Russia for a century. This included Armenian and Cherkessk auxiliaries from Crimea, along with other minor vassal forces. There was also a contingent of experienced Genoese mercenaries from their trading centre of Caffa in Crimea. However, the core of his *ordu*, his army, was made up of Mongol-Tatar cavalry, and, even after reversals such as the defeat at Vozha two years earlier, these were soldiers still with a formidable – literally fearsome – reputation.

Mamai's failure adequately to scout the Russian advance meant that, while he had a rough idea of the strength and composition of Dmitry's army, he was having to guess at their disposition on the field. As it was, he rightly assumed (with the exception of the Ambush Regiment, of which he was dangerously unaware) that Dmitry would have to be essentially conservative, given the composite nature of his army. Likewise, Mamai adopted the classic Mongol-Tatar five-regiment model, with a scout screen, a vanguard of heavy cavalry, a force of lighter cavalry behind, and flying columns to the left and right, the so-called 'east' and 'west', respectively, regardless of the actual orientation of the battlefield, because by tradition an *ordu* would encamp facing south. The Genoese professionals, who had a reputation for being steady in battle, he placed at the centre of his front line, to anchor the wings of less reliable infantry, mixed with horse. This would also allow Mamai to use his cavalry more freely, with a force of heavy Mongol-Tatar veterans kept in reserve, ready to exploit the inevitable breaks in the Russian line. Ultimately, he felt that numbers and ferocity would carry the day – and he was almost right.

THE BATTLE

'Each of you should now be ready, because in the morning it will be impossible to prepare, as our guests are already approaching. They are standing by the river at Nepriadva, they have been prepared for battle near Kulikovo Field, and in the morning we will be drinking from the same cup as them.' (Grand Prince Dmitry to his troops.)

The Tale of the Rout of Mamai

The battle itself took place over some four hours one Saturday, beginning with a legendary clash of champions as morning fogs cleared, ending with a prolonged and murderous chase, as Russians rode down Mamai's fleeing troops. Yet while it turned out to be a victory for Grand Prince Dmitry, even if a very costly one, for most of those four hours it looked as if his enemies would take the day. This was a battle won not by numbers (where the invaders had the edge), nor by skill or armaments (as in this, both were evenly matched) but by tactics – and a good deal of luck.

Alexander Bubnov's *Morning on the Kulikovo Field in 1380* gives a good sense of the heterogeneity of Dmitry's infantry forces, often made up of a ragtag collection of local militias, city guards, and the lesser retainers of nobles. (Photo by Fine Art Images/ Heritage Images/Getty Images)

This 19th-century painting by Józéf Brandt shows a 14th- or 15th-century Polish-Lithuanian aristocratic cavalryman, of the kind which would have made up the elite of Jogaila's forces. Note the eastern-style curved sabre but also the warhammer, better suited to punching through the plate mail worn in the west. (Public domain)

DMITRY ACROSS THE DON

'Grand Duke Dmitry Ivanovich… gathered many warriors and went against the Tatars in order to protect his patrimonies, the holy churches, Christianity, and all the Russian lands. When the prince crossed the Oka, other messages came to him, that Mamai had gathered his troops behind the Don, and was camped in the field and waiting for Jogaila and the Lithuanian army.

'The Grand Duke crossed the Don, to where there is a clean and spacious field. There, the filthy Polovtsi, the regiments of Tatars, gathered in an open field near the mouth of the Nepriadva.'

The *Short Chronicle Tale*

Dmitry set out from Moscow in August 1380, heading south-east to the tributary city of Kolomna, held by Mikula Vasilievich Velyaminov, where most of his host was assembled. After inspecting them at Devichye (Maidens') Field, he then marched them west towards Serpukhov. There, on the 26th, on the north bank of the Oka River, he met up with Vladimir Andreyevich and the forces he had mustered, and also late-arriving detachments, which had followed at speed from Moscow, under Dmitry's seasoned seneschal of the city, Timofei Velyaminov (a cousin of Mikula of Kolomna). 'What makes a noise that rattles early before dawn?' asked *The Zadonschina*. 'It is Prince Vladimir Andreyevich's regiments as he leads them to the Great Don.'

The combined force headed south along the Old Dankovskaya Road, and on 6 September reached the Don. By this time, spies and scouts had reported not just that Mamai was camped on the watershed south of the Don, at Kulikovo, but that Jogaila's Lithuanian army was marching eastwards from Odoyev and would arrive by 10 September at the latest. Oleg of Ryazan's forces were approaching from the north-east, but at a much more relaxed pace and were unlikely to arrive before the 14th, which was the last day Mamai had set for a muster of his combined army. For this intelligence, Dmitry could thank Semyon Melik, a Moscow boyar of Lithuanian extraction, who was seemingly the closest thing he had to a chief of intelligence. He participated personally in reconnaissance missions before the battle, scouting out the land before Dmitry led his army across the Oka, and later bringing information on the location and strength of Mamai's forces. In the words of *The Tale of the Rout of Mamai*, Dmitry sent 'the best of his heroes to the field to meet with the Tatar scouts on the steppe: Semyon Melik, Ignaty Kren, Fom Tynin, Pyotr Gorsky, Karp Oleksin, Petrush Churikov and many other far riders.' In this way, as in so many others, the Russians had learned the Mongols' arts of war, including the use of far-ranging patrols tasked not just with scouting the enemy lines but also acquiring what they called 'tongues'. In other words, they captured at least one soldier from Mamai's army (presumably a sentry, scout or forager) who could be interrogated for the intelligence he could reveal.

The news was grim. Even without his allies from Lithuania and Ryazan, Mamai had assembled a powerful army, mobilizing the full military might of the Blue Horde. On the other hand, Dmitry still seemed to have surprise on his side. A noble prisoner snatched from the enemy – presumably again Semyon Melik's work – said that Mamai is 'already standing on Kuzmin Gati, but he is in no hurry, he is waiting for Olgerd of Lithuania and Oleg of Ryazan, but the king does not know about your army, nor does he expect you to meet with him, according to a message from Oleg, for another three days until he is over the Don.' Although the etymology of 'Kuzmin Gati' is disputed, it presumably referred to the plains around the Red Hill, as the only place today known to be called Kuzmin Gatya is a village near Tambov, some 200km (125 miles) away to the east.

So even though the Golden Horde's army was already larger than his own, Dmitry opted to strike before Mamai could be reinforced by his approaching allies. He encamped at Berezouy, on the north bank of the Don and north-east of Mamai's forces and on 7 September held a council of war. Ostensibly to agree on their tactics, in keeping with the democratic traditions of the Rus', in practice this was likely to have been, more than anything else, a chance for the young Grand Prince to ensure the egos and rivalries amongst his princely allies were respectively satisfied and defused. He presented the situation in stark terms: the Don was their Rubicon, once they crossed it, they were committed, and had to fight, fight at once, and fight to win. Some of those assembled lost their nerve and advocated withdrawal. Others encouraged Dmitry to remain on their side of the river and wait for Mamai to come to them. With Jogaila nearing, though, and a solid array of Muscovite client princes in his pocket, Dmitry had both common sense and a political bloc on his side and he won the day. Late on the 7th, the Russian forces forded the Don, and early on the next morning began to deploy. The battle had begun.

Ernst Lissner's 1907 watercolour depicts the legendary scene where Grand Prince Dmitry seeks out the Orthodox monk Sergius of Radonezh for his blessing. (Public domain)

OVER THE DON

'By the beginning of the second hour [of daylight], the horns on both sides were getting louder, Tatar and Russian horns were blowing harder. The men-at-arms were not seen yet, for the morning was foggy, but the earth was moving terrifyingly in the east to the sea, and Kulikovo Field was bending towards the Don in the west. The rivers were reaching out of their beds, for never had such numbers of people been in that place.'

The Tale of the Rout of Mamai

The chronicles all assert that, before the battle, early that fateful morning, Dmitry addressed his forces and presented their mission in religious rather than political terms. According to the *Novgorod First Chronicle*, he told them: 'brothers, God is our refuge and our strength.' While perhaps inevitable in chronicles written and kept by religious authorities, this is also likely true. There was then no real sense of Russian nationalism as such; instead, their Orthodox faith was probably the most powerful binding force amongst the disparate contingents. They fought under banners depicting the Virgin Mary – whose feast day was 8 September – and patron saints, notably St George and St Andrew, guardians of Moscow and Russia, respectively. They marched to battle singing hymns and common songs with religious themes. Both because of his genuine faith, a product of Alexei's tutoring, and also his political instincts, Dmitry had long cultivated his alliance with the Orthodox Church. Having won the blessing of Sergius of Radonezh beforehand, public displays of piety were not just ways to enthuse an army that knew the odds were stacked against it, they were also ways of demonstrating that alliance for future advantage.

As per Dmitry's plan, his forces formed up on the field in three-line order. The Sentry Regiment stretched a screen of Russian and Mongol-Tatar scouts along the front of the army. The Mongol-Tatar mercenaries were under the governor of Pereyaslavl, Andrei Serkizov, himself of Tatar

origins. Indeed, one of the reasons Dmitry had placed his own man, Mikhail Ivanovich Akinfov, in command of the regiment was likely the potentially prickly relations between Serkizov and Prince Semyon Konstantinovich of Obolensk, who led his own personal retinue in the regiment. There were also detachments from Galich and Tarusa, possibly infantry levies, under Mstislav Konstantinovich, prince of Tarusa.

The Advance Regiment was a more substantial force, largely infantry, although some noblemen and their personal retinues were mounted. It was led by Mikula Vasilievich Velyaminov, the governor of Kolomna. While some accounts also place Lithuanians in the Regiment of the Right Hand, and Dmitry Olgerdovich and his men on the Left Hand, it actually appears that they began the battle in the Advance Regiment. When this vanguard was broken, the brothers were split, and joined the units on each flank.

The Main Regiment formed up on either side of Dmitry's personal detachment. Mikhail Brenok, resplendent in the Grand Prince's armour, took his place at the centre, beneath the banners of the Virgin Mary and of St George (patron saint of Moscow), even while the real Dmitry inconspicuously moved into place towards the centre of the unit, flanked by aides ready to pass on his orders. 'If I die, it will be among you,' he reportedly told the soldiers around him, and 'if I live, it will be while fighting amongst you, too,' demonstrating the time-honoured politician's knack of making self-interest sound self-sacrificing.

This substantial, essentially mounted formation was made up of detachments from Dmitrov, Kostroma, Uglich, Vladimir (a large force under Muscovite boyar Timofey Vasilievich Valui), Vyazemsk (under Prince Ivan V), Yuriyev-Polsky, Kostroma (under governor Ivan Rodionovich Kvashnya) and Zvenigorod. However, the largest elements were from Moscow and Beloözero. Prince Fyodor of Beloözero and his son Ivan were amongst the first to heed Dmitry's muster, but they and most of their heavy cavalry would die in the battle. Timofei Velyaminov was in tactical command of the Main Regiment, while Dmitry himself sought to control the battlefield.

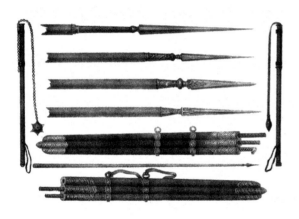

This etching clearly shows the characteristic triangular heads of Russian spears, as well as samples of maces and darts (Public domain)

The Main Regiment's flanks were protected by the smaller Regiments of the Left and Right Hand, also mounted formations. Blocking the gap between the main forces and the woody banks of the Nizhny Dubik and Smolka rivers, their role was to prevent the Mongol-Tatar horse from being able to outflank Dmitry's army. The main strength of the Regiment of the Right Hand was made up of a detachment from Kolomna, under Nikolai Velyaminov, along with a small force from Polotsk and a larger one from Rostov under Andrei Fedorovich, as well as Prince Fyodor of Yeletsky and his personal retainers. As noted above, contrary to some accounts, Andrei Olgerdovich was not in command of this regiment, but instead joined it during the battle. Likewise, Dmitry Olgerdovich did not lead the Regiment of the Left Hand, which was actually largely made up of the Yaroslavl detachment under their Prince Vasily Vasilievich, who captained the regiment, supported by men from Mozhaisk under their Prince Fyodor Mikhailovich.

Some sources suggest there was also a Reserve, even if no more than a couple of small detachments of mixed provenance, which was placed to the west and rear of the Guard Regiment. If this was the case, the fact that they were relatively small forces, and made up of scraps and strays from other detachments who had not fought together and had no prestigious captain, suggests little was expected of them. They may have been there primarily to reassure Mamai and try to ensure he had no suspicions about the real reserve represented by the Ambush Regiment. However, as discussed below, it is more likely that there was no specific Reserve (and certainly the absence of any record of a commander for the unit implies that this was the case). Instead it was a scratch force thrown together of stragglers who had made their way back from the front line, when Mongol-Tatar forces looked as if they were about to break through to the rear.

The Ambush Regiment was the real reserve, one that took full advantage of the morning fogs to take position in the oak woods to the east (or conceivably behind them with an eye to swooping round the edge of the thickets). It was a powerful all-cavalry force, largely made up of Vladimir Alexeyevich's troops from Serpukhov, battle-hardened veterans in the main, supported by detachments from Kashira, Murom, Novosilsk and Yelets. Prince Vladimir was in command, but closely advised by Dmitry Bobrok-Volinsky. Alongside him rode Roman Mikhailovich of Bryansk, Vasily Mikhailovich of Kashira, and Roman Semyonovich of Novosilsk.

READYING MAMAI'S HOST

'And after a few days [Mamai] crossed the great Volga River with all his strength, and added many other hordes to his great army and said to them: "Let us go to the Russian land and get rich from Russian gold!" So the godless went to Russia, like a roaring lion, like a spiteful viper.'

The Tale of the Rout of Mamai

Meanwhile, Mamai's forces appear to have been caught uncharacteristically napping. Despite a strong tradition of launching far-ranging cavalry patrols to detect enemy movements, this time the Mongol-Tatars seem to have been complacent, for reasons we still do not know. In the early morning, the Golden Horde's soldiers were rising as usual, still recovering from their days of march, when it became clear that the Russians were assembling on the north of the plain, under cover of fog. Nonetheless, most of these were professional soldiers, and while Mamai had not anticipated Dmitry's arrival quite so soon, he had made his plans. The fact that he, too, had adopted a conventional, linear disposition for his forces, again for reasons of both flexibility and familiarity, meant that his army could quickly deploy for battle.

Behind his own screen of light cavalry outriders, both Mongol-Tatars and Circassians, he placed an especially solid front line made up of veteran Mongol-Tatar heavy cavalry flanking a core company of Genoese heavy infantry. Mixing cavalry and infantry in this way contradicted the usual practices of the Golden Horde, but likely reflected Mamai's understanding that this was likely to be a close-quarters brawl more than a battle of manoeuvre. Overall commander of this first battle line was, according to some Russian accounts, a Tatar general called Telyak or Tulyak. According to usual Mongol-Tatar practice, these regiments were drawn up in five ranks, with wide gaps between each *zuut* to allow the lighter cavalry behind to interpenetrate if an opportunity to scour the enemy with arrows appeared.

This representation of Dmitry Donskoy, from the 'Millennium of Russia' Monument in Novgorod, emphasizes his role as a crusader, defending Orthodoxy from Islam. (© Dar Veter)

Close behind them were four large regiments of mixed Mongol-Tatar horse and foot, with auxiliaries on each flank. To the west was a regiment of Armenian infantry and cavalry, to the east, Circassians, with a few Armenian infantry and archers in support. This structure, with two heavy echelons of forces, underlined Mamai's intent to make this a battle of impact and attrition, rather than manoeuvre and finesse.

THE START OF THE BATTLE

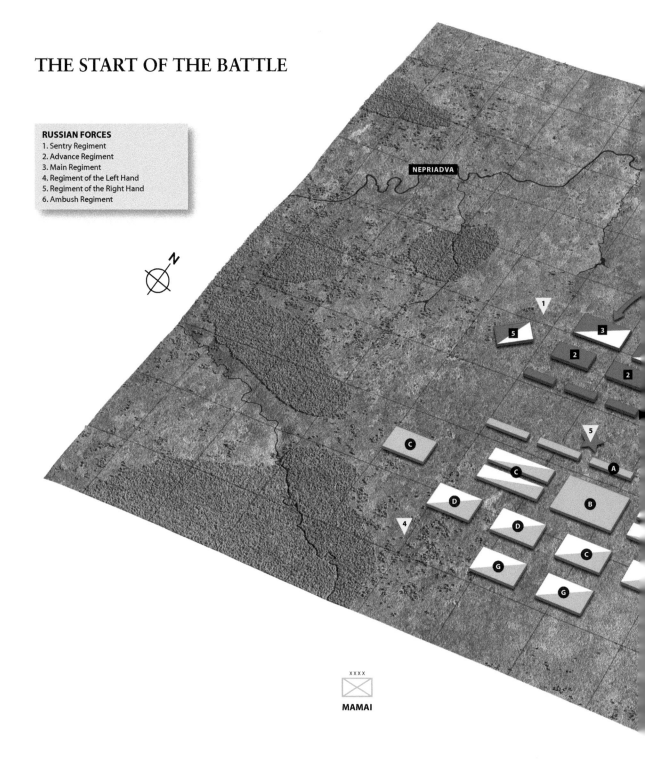

RUSSIAN FORCES
1. Sentry Regiment
2. Advance Regiment
3. Main Regiment
4. Regiment of the Left Hand
5. Regiment of the Right Hand
6. Ambush Regiment

NEPRIADVA

MAMAI

EVENTS

1. The Dmitry deploys his forces in two lines behind a scout screen.

2. The Ambush Regiment deploys under cover of fog.

3. Mamai establishes his command position atop the Red Hill.

4. The Golden Horde forces deployed with an especially strong advance detachment of infantry flanked by heavy cavalry.

5. At the outset of the battle, myth has it that respective champions fight between the lines, both dying.

xxxx
DMITRY

GOLDEN HORDE FORCES
A. Scouts
B. Infantry, including Genoese heavy foot
C. Mongol heavy cavalry
D. Mongol light cavalry
E. Regiment of the East
F. Regiment of the West
G. Reserves
H. Genoese infantry

TATINKI
FORD

RUSSIAN
CAMP

DON

2

3

6

2

4

SMOLKA

F

H

3

Note: Gridlines are shown at intervals of 1km (0.6 miles)

Mikhail Avilov's iconic picture of the duel between Peresvet and the Golden Horde's champion, Chelubey, before the battle. (Photo by Fine Art Images/Heritage Images/Getty Images)

Behind were two regiments of Mongol-Tatar cavalry in reserve. Mamai established himself atop the flat-topped Red Hill to the east, from where he could watch the battle in (presumed) safety and use black and white flags or couriers to transmit his orders across the battlefield. Unlike Grand Prince Dmitry, Mamai had no intention of getting involved in the actual fighting, but this should not necessarily be considered a mark of timidity; it was not the Golden Horde's custom for a general to fight, not least because he had to maintain his overall control of the battle. This was long-standing practice; Friar Carpini, who travelled amongst the Mongols in the 13th century, noted that their commanders 'stayed a long way from the enemy'. That said, Mamai did not rely just on distance to keep him safe. A contingent of Genoese heavy infantry was also positioned around the base of the hill for his own security, a precaution that proved wise in the circumstances.

THE BATTLE OF CHAMPIONS

'[T]here was a thick mist covering the earth: that mist stayed until the third hour [of daylight]. And the Lord told the mist to clear and bestowed the emergence of light... And the latches of death were opened, the earth was trembling, and the troops, collected from far away, from east and west, were seized by terror.'

The *Expanded Chronicle Tale*

Both sides sought to probe the other's deployments and intentions, but the early morning fog precluded most of such intelligence gathering. A few skirmishes broke out when rival bands of scouts stumbled onto each other in the murk, and Melik was forced to thunder back to the Russian lines after one such sortie, a file of angry Mongols at his heels. Essentially the battle remained on hold until the autumn sun began to thin the fog. When it cleared

at around 11 o'clock in the morning, both armies cautiously advanced and braced themselves for the confrontation. By all accounts, the Golden Horde's forces, crossing the low ridge of the watershed, made a particularly grand show, sunlight glittering on spear points, the air filled with the bray of trumpets and the thunder of *naccaras*, great kettle drums typically borne on the backs of camels. According to the *Novgorod First Chronicle*, on seeing the size of Mamai's forces, some of the more inexperienced Russian forces, probably levies from the western cities, even fled the field. Ironically enough, this may well not have done them much good; some German chronicles say that Jogaila's forces fell on the Russians after the battle as they headed back home and wiped them out, but the Russian chronicles provide scant corroboration, and it may be that the deserters encountered the Lithuanians and suffered the consequences.

Although it is entirely possible this is simply a colourful apocryphal tale, the convention is that, in a clash evocative of older times, champions from each side met and duelled in the no man's land between armies before the battle. The Russians were represented by the warrior-monk Alexander Peresvet. Born of a boyar family from Bryansk, Peresvet was a disciple of Sergius of Radonezh and he, along with another nobleman-turned-monk,

THE INITIAL CLASH

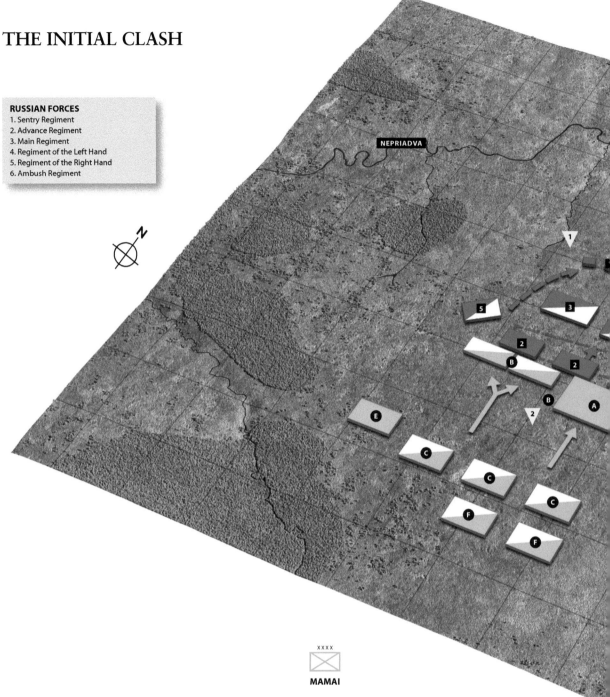

RUSSIAN FORCES
1. Sentry Regiment
2. Advance Regiment
3. Main Regiment
4. Regiment of the Left Hand
5. Regiment of the Right Hand
6. Ambush Regiment

NEPRIADVA

MAMAI

EVENTS

1. The Russian Sentry Regiment is swept away by the Golden Horde's scout screen; some stragglers join the Advance Regiment, others regroup at the rear of the army.

2. The Golden Horde's main battle line engages; the Russian Advance Regiment advances slightly to meet it.

3. The Advance Regiment is pushed back by the Golden Horde's weight of numbers, especially on its eastern flank. The Russian battle line slowly pivots.

4. Mamai sends a unit of Mongol light cavalry sweeping round the battleline to engage the eastern flank of the Advance Regiment.

5. The Regiment of the Left Hand advances slightly to threaten the Mongol reinforcements, but cannot engage lest it open up the entire Russian flank to Mamai's cavalry.

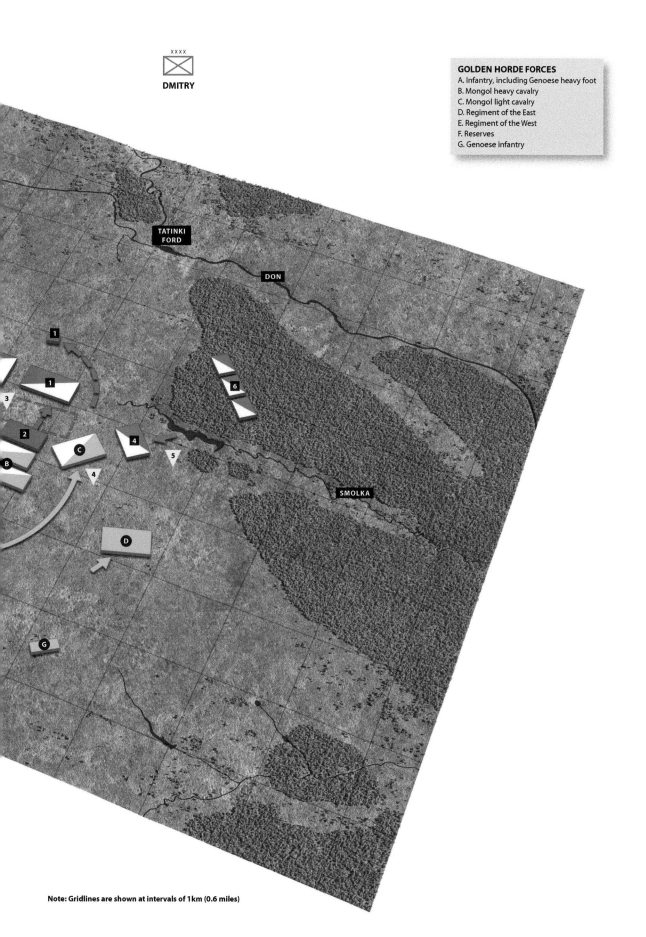

xxxx

DMITRY

GOLDEN HORDE FORCES
A. Infantry, including Genoese heavy foot
B. Mongol heavy cavalry
C. Mongol light cavalry
D. Regiment of the East
E. Regiment of the West
F. Reserves
G. Genoese infantry

TATINKI
FORD

DON

SMOLKA

Note: Gridlines are shown at intervals of 1km (0.6 miles)

Rodion Oslabya, joined Dmitry's entourage as a religious duty, at Sergius' behest. While Russia did not have religious knightly orders such as the Western crusaders, their boyar background meant they had been raised as warriors. Against Peresvet the Mongol-Tatars fielded Chelubey (some accounts name him Temir-Murza or Tavrulom), a veteran warrior famed for his physical prowess and combat skills alike, a wrestler and horseman almost as broad as he was tall.

They fought on horseback, with spears, and, according to the tale, in the first pass, each killed the other. However, Chelubey's body was knocked clean off his horse, while Peresvet's corpse stayed in the saddle, at least for a while. The Russians chose to regard it as a good omen, which may as much as anything else say something about the triumph of optimism and their eagerness to find some comfort in this reciprocal killing. Peresvet was later made an Orthodox saint, and the words attributed to him in the *Zadonshchina*: 'it is better that we perish by our own swords, than end up in the power of the pagans,' became something of a recurring theme in the chronicles. Whether or not he existed, an apple-wood staff meant to have been his is still on display in the Ryazan kremlin local history museum, and his name remains widely known in Russia to this day.

THE INITIAL CLASH

'On the field, the mighty soldiers were fighting, swords reflecting a bloody glow; there was a great clatter and noise from the breaking of spears, such that it was not possible to hear or watch that terrible and bitter hour, when so many thousands of God's creations were ended.'

The Tale of the Rout of Mamai

Mamai clearly wanted to make up for lost time. His advance guard swept away the light cavalry screen and scouts of the Sentry Regiment. At this point, atypically, this was largely an infantry battle, as Mamai deployed Mongol-Tatar footmen, supported with crossbow fire from the Genoese behind them, in an apparent hope that they could push the Russian screen back to past the Smolka River and in the process clear the way to the relatively open grassland beyond. Then, he could unleash his cavalry to fullest effect. The small Russian force was neither able nor expected to hold back Mamai's initial strike, although the fighting, while brief, was bitter. By all accounts Mikhail Akinfov died very early in the battle, as well as Prince Mstislav of Tarusa and Andrei Serkizov the former Tatar – the first but not the last commanders to fall. Soon, the Sentry Regiment was forced to fall back in good order to join the Advance Regiment behind. The infantry elements likely moved to the very rear of the Russian army, and may have been the basis for the reserve deployed later in the afternoon.

In response, Mamai pushed his own vanguard forward to engage, including the heavy footmen of the Genoese contingent at the centre. At first this remained largely an infantry struggle, as the Golden Horde's troops sought to push the Advance Regiment far enough back to open a route for their cavalry to flank the Russians on their left. After no more than an hour's hard fighting, they were successful in pivoting the Russian line enough that Mamai decided to send in cavalry from his right-flank force,

This 17th-century miniature of the battle, made for a copy of *The Tale of the Rout of Mamai*, underscores how similar the two armies must have looked, beyond the sabres in Mongol-Tatar hands and the straight swords of the Russians. (Public domain)

past the Smolka. A few of them infiltrated the gap between Dmitry's Advance and Main Regiments. Although they are likely to have been easy pickings for Russian archers while exposed between the formations, most instead slammed into the flank of the Advance Regiment.

Dmitry moved his Regiment of the Left Hand slightly forward in support, but the pressure of the infantry onslaught from the front and cavalry charges to its flanks proved too much for the Advance Regiment. Mikula Velyaminov of Kolomna fell in the fighting and, with his death, the formation began to break apart. The regiment was forced to withdraw, by detachments rather than en masse, although this was managed again in relatively good order – a retreat, but not a rout. Some of the footmen joined the other regiments behind, more filtered to the rear. Andrei and Dmitry Olgerdovich and their retinues had been separated in the fighting, but they peeled off and managed to join the Regiment of the Right and the Left Hand, respectively. The preliminaries were over, and the butchery proper was about to start.

THE FALL OF THE FALSE DMITRY (PP. 62–63)

Infuriated by the Russian resistance, Mamai unleashes the full force of his cavalry against the Main Regiment, above all seeking the death of Prince Dmitry – not knowing that the Russians' commander's armour is being worn by young Brenok, a subterfuge aided by the full-face mask of his helmet. It is perhaps inevitable that the false Dmitry (1), marked out by his princely regalia and his personal banner, will fall. To his left is one of the Lithuanian knights (2) who followed the Olgerdoviches into the lands of the Rus'. The Mongol forces are a mix of horse archers (3) and heavy lancers (4), although note that even the latter also carry the distinctive composite bow. Fortunately for Dmitry, when Bobrok fell, the banner of Moscow (5) was saved, and this helped him rally the troops when news of the supposed prince's death shook the resolve of the Russian army.

This picture is from the opening of the Kulikovo Field museum in 2016. The Russians' lamellar armour is clearly visible on the figure at the fore. (Photo by Stanislav Krasilnikov\TASS via Getty Images)

BATTLE IS JOINED

'And then the great army of Mamai moved, all the forces of the Tatars. And on our part, the Great Prince Dmitry Ivanovich with all the princes of Russia, gathering their regiments, went against the filthy Polovtsians [Mongol-Tatars] with all their warriors.'

The *Expanded Chronicle Tale*

Mamai's infantry were exhausted and they did not immediately follow up. Indeed, the commander of his vanguard appears not to have wanted or been ordered to do so, and this helped the survivors of the Advance Regiment to disengage. By around noon, or a little after, the Golden Horde had been able to push beyond the Smolka, and was now facing the Russian Main Regiment, with Dmitry – seemingly – at their head, flanked by his personal retinue.

At this point Mamai could at last unleash his heavy cavalry, who charged from each wing of the front line. They opened with the usual storm of arrows, and Dmitry's ploy of using a double proved a cunning one, as they concentrated their fire on his banner, and then focused their charge there. Brenok was, after all, hard to miss, standing in gleaming armour between two flags: Moscow's with a mounted St George bearing a spear in white on red, and Grand Prince Dmitry's, a darker banner bearing a golden image of Jesus' face.

The charging cavalry must have been a fearsome sight, as the front ranks, still at the gallop, put aside their bows for spears, swords and maces. The Russian cavalry of the Main Regiment may have tried to launch a countercharge, but the battlefield was too small to allow them to build up much momentum. The heavy infantry braced their spears and hunched behind their large, kite shields, awaiting the shock of impact.

A re-enactor playing the role of a boyar heavy cavalryman, in scale mail and semi-conical helmet. Note his metal vambraces and the characteristically colourful shield in the left of the shot. (© Petr Shelomovskiy)

By all accounts Brenok and his personal guards, including Prince Fyodor Romanovich of Beloözero, Dmitry's brother-in-law, and the scout Semyon Melik, put up a hard fight, striking down their foes 'as if they were felling timber, or mowing grass with a scythe.' However, theirs was an untenable situation. Ultimately the Mongol-Tatars' determination to reach him and the storm of arrows still arcing in above the heads of the front-line fighters made the outcome inevitable. The clash quickly devolved into a vicious, no-quarters mêlée, and, in the words of one chronicle, blood 'flowed, as if in a cloudburst.' Brenok fell (along with Prince Fyodor and Melik), and word of the death of 'Prince Dmitry' began to spread through the Russian ranks. The extent to which this whole coalition had been summoned and bound by one man's will, authority and political machinations became clear as the army wavered. (According to some accounts, this may actually have been when some levies deserted.)

However, the real prince quickly revealed himself, and his banner, which had been saved from the indignity of capture, was brought to him. He was able to rally the army before the rumours of his death, greatly exaggerated, did too much harm. Dmitry may have been cautious, but he was no coward, and he then threw himself into the battle, flanked by his relieved knights.

The Main Regiment had suffered serious losses, and both the Regiments of the Left and Right Hand were now also engaged. However, in their eagerness to strike at the false prince, the Mongols also made two potential errors. First of all, by throwing their main force straight into the mêlée, they had limited their opportunities to take advantage of their strengths in manoeuvre and archery (even if, in fairness, the Russians may well have been their match by this stage) and instead turned this into the kind of close-quarter brawl in which the Russians excelled. Secondly, in their charge towards Dmitry's own position, the Mongol-Tatar cavalry outdistanced and cut in front of the heavy Genoese infantry. They had been placed in the centre of the front line, opposite the Grand Prince's detachment, precisely to be a powerful striking force. Now, though, the Genoese were forced to split up, with elements moving to the left and the right, and their crossbows were of limited value once enemy and ally were snarled up in the mêlée.

A BLOODY AFTERNOON

'The bravery of many thousand warriors was witnessed, each trying to outdo the other, and all seeking to win the glory of victory. Spears were broken like straw, arrows fell like rain, and the dust blocked the sun's rays, and only the swords flashed like lightning. And people fell, like hay under a scythe, and blood flowed like water in streams.'

V.N. Tatishchev's retelling of the *Nikon Chronicle*

Nonetheless, the Golden Horde had numbers on its side and thus the capacity to cycle fresh troops into the battle. Besides, accounts spoke of a strong wind from the south that at this time was blowing into the Russians' faces, blinding them with dust and sending their arrows off course. What followed was an hour or more of murderous back and forth, as the cavalry which were now dominating the front lines of both armies were forced into a pattern of brief, local attacks, followed by a pause to regroup and a return to the fight. This was bloody, vicious, confused and confusing, with little sense of tactics or finesse. As the *Nikon Chronicle* put it, 'such a battle was raging that it was impossible to tell whether the Tatars were coming for Russian troops, or the Russians for Tatar troops.'

The battlefield was strewn with the bodies of dead and dying men and horses, the air full of the beating of drums, the bray of horns, and the cries of the wounded. Indeed, one chronicle says that such was the clamour that it was impossible to hear the words or commands of others, even if they were next in the fighting line. The battle was now being fought across the whole line from the Dubik to the Smolka. Even allowing for the inevitable exaggerations, Grand Prince Dmitry was fighting hard: he would have two horses killed under him, and by the end of the battle all his bodyguards were dead or wounded. The *Expanded Chronicle Tale* presents him as a veritable superhero: 'And how many times he was struck on the right or the left by the soldiers, who surrounded him, like a sea, on all sides! And how many blows struck him on the head, and on his shoulders, and in his body, but God defended him on the day of battle with a shield of truth and with a weapon of good will'. Nonetheless, although the ebb and flow meant that the Russians were sometimes in the ascendant, they were being pushed back, slowly but surely.

Sergei Kirillov's *Kulikovo Field* (1990) is a typical modern representation that emphasizes the differences between the Mongol-Tatar horse archer and the Russian spearman, although in practice there were many similarities between the fighting styles and equipment of the two sides. (© Sergei Kirillov)

THE AMBUSH SPRUNG

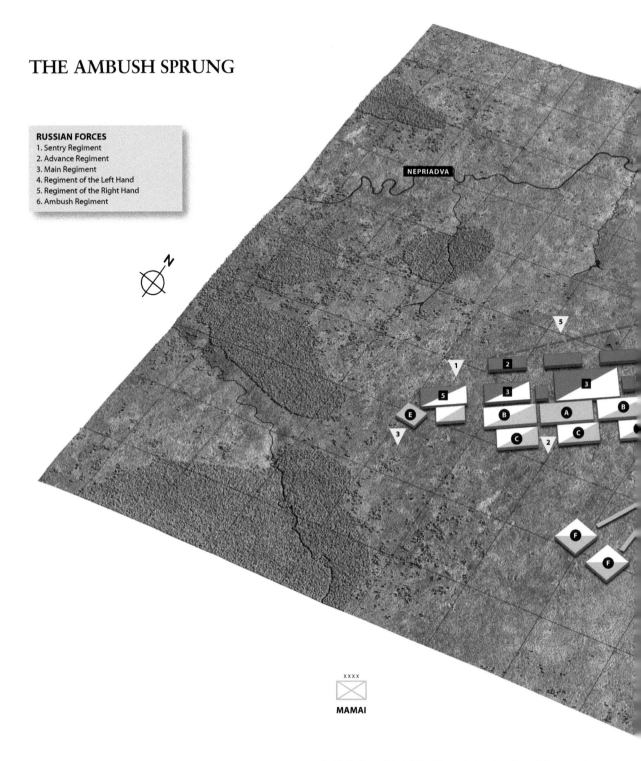

RUSSIAN FORCES
1. Sentry Regiment
2. Advance Regiment
3. Main Regiment
4. Regiment of the Left Hand
5. Regiment of the Right Hand
6. Ambush Regiment

NEPRIADVA

MAMAI

EVENTS

1. The Advance Regiment falls back, joining and reinforcing the Main Regiment.

2. The Golden Horde heavy cavalry converge on the false Dmitry, splitting the Genoese Infantry. Brenok is killed, but the real prince is able to prevent a rout. The battle becomes an increasingly chaotic melee.

3. The Regiment of the East, reinforced by Mongol light cavalry from Mamai's second line, engage the Russian's Regiment of the Right Hand. The other Mongol light cavalry join the main melee.

4. The Regiment of the Left Hand is increasingly embattled, especially as some of the Circassians from the Regiment of the West ford the Smolka and attack it from the flank.

5. The main force of the Russian army is slowly pushed back and round, leaving its flank increasingly vulnerable.

6. Spotting the opportunity for which he had hoped, Mamai sends his last reserves, supported by elements of the Regiment of the West, round to attack the exposed Russian flank.

7. Before this force can reach its objective, it is taken by surprise and in its flank as the Ambush Regiment charges from the Wood of Green Oaks, breaking the enemy detachment.

XXXX
DMITRY

GOLDEN HORDE FORCES
A. Infantry, including Genoese heavy foot
B. Mongol heavy cavalry
C. Mongol light cavalry
D. Regiment of the East
E. Regiment of the West
F. Reserves
G. Genoese infantry

TATINKI FORD

DON

SMOLKA

Note: Gridlines are shown at intervals of 1km (0.6 miles)

By one o'clock, the Russian line was beginning to break. As gaps began to open in the Main Regiment and between it and the Regiments of the Left and Right Hands, Mamai could throw troops through them to close with the often much less-experienced forces in the Russian second line. In a desperate bid to prevent the enemy from acquiring battlefield momentum, Gleb of Bryansk (according to *The Tale of Mamai's Rout*; other sources claim Gleb was not at Kulikovo, suggesting it was another prince) gathered around himself a force of heavy cavalry, largely men from Vladimir who had been pushed back from the Main Regiment, along with some stragglers from the Advance Regiment. At their head, he launched a counter-attack along the left flank of the Main Regiment, 'through the corpses of the dead.' This briefly stabilized the situation and allowed the Regiment of the Left Hand to rally, but Gleb then fell to enemy arrows, and soon the counthercharge was spent. Exposed, his force was vulnerable not just to Mongol-Tatar and Armenian archers, but Genoese professionals who at last had a clear target for their murderous crossbows.

So, the bloody grind continued. The Regiment of the Right Hand under Nikolai Velyaminov managed to hold the line, but the Regiment of the Left Hand was looking increasingly vulnerable, not least as some Golden Horde footmen (possible dismounted Circassians) sifted through the woods on the banks of the Smolka, crossed the river, and posed a threat to the regiment's rear. Timofey Valui of Uglich fell, and as the Regiment of the Left Hand retreated, the whole Russian line was now in effect being slowly pivoted round its centre of gravity. With the prospect of his enemy being either broken or pinned against the Nepriadva, Mamai – as Dmitry had anticipated – doubled down, seeing a breakthrough on the east as the key to victory. He concentrated his forces on that flank, throwing in all the troops he had left in reserve, a combination of Mongol-Tatar cavalry and foot, with some Armenian archers and Circassians. More to the point, as the Russian Main Regiment was forced to fall back and round in response, detachments of Mongol-Tatar heavy cavalry in the centre of the battle acquired some room to manoeuvre, and some moved east to seek to exploit the opportunity.

The hard fighting continued. On the eastern flank, with no clear open ground thanks to the broken scrubland along the Smolka's banks, there was even less scope for anything other than a shoving, swirling scrum, with horses trampling bodies into the mud, and blood washing into the river. The Russians fought hard, but they were exhausted and they felt their defeat upon them. By around two o'clock in the afternoon, the Regiment of the Left Hand was fragmenting, and the Mongol-Tatar forces had a clear route round into the Russians' rear.

AMBUSH!

'And then there came the eighth hour of the day, when the south wind blew from behind us, and Volynets loudly called: "Prince Vladimir, our time has come, and the hour has come!" And he added: "My brothers, my friends, be bold: the power of the holy spirit is with us!"

And his friends and companions sprang from the green oak, as if they were falcons… and their banners were directed by that doughty general Dmitry Volynets; and they were like David's children, whose hearts were like lions, like fierce wolves amongst a flock of sheep, and they began to slaughter the Tatars without mercy.'

The Tale of the Rout of Mamai

Seeing the Russian left flank withdrawing, and eager to seize an opportunity to pin Dmitry and roll round the remnants of the army at the centre, Mongol-Tatar units broke through. At this point, according to one chronicle, Lithuanian prince Andrei Olgerdovich, broke and fled at the sight of yet more regiments of Mongol-Tatar soldiers appearing at the rear of the Russian lines. He ran for the Nepriadva River at the rear, chased by Tatars. Nonetheless, he made it to safety, However, given that it was actually his brother Dmitry who did not survive Kulikovo, and little account exists of his end, it may well be that the chronicle simply confused the princes. After all, it was on the left, where Dmitry Olgerdovich was, that Mamai was sending his remaining fresh forces.

A reserve force, largely of infantry formerly from the Sentry and Advance Regiments, wheeled to try and block this new threat, but a few hundred tired and scared footmen could not provide much of a defence for the Russian rear. They did not have to, though. For this was precisely the situation Dmitry had anticipated when he stationed his Ambush Regiment, a force of his best boyar cavalry, in the Wood of Green Oaks to the east. By all accounts, this was an advantage that could so easily have been wasted, with the hotter-headed Prince Vladimir Andreyevich being repeatedly counselled to patience by Dmitry Mikhailovich Bobrok-Volinsky, who was likely his technical subordinate, but in practice was speaking with Grand Prince Dmitry's voice. *The Tale of the Rout of Mamai* recounts how, as the battle had begun to turn against the Russians and their casualties mounted, he kept wanting to join the fray:

Seeing the same death of the Russian sons, Prince Vladimir Andreyevich could not restrain himself. 'So what's the use of standing by in our situation?' he snarled, 'What good are we doing? Who are we helping? Already our princes and our boyars, all our Russian sons are being massacred,' but Bobrok-Volinsky replied, 'The situation, oh prince, is dire, but our time has not yet come... We must bear this a little longer, until the time is right and at that hour we will give our enemies what they deserve.'

The soldiers themselves – members of a feudal warrior class raised to believe bravery to be the highest virtue, even at the expense of tactical finesse – echoed the prince's plaints. They wept bitter tears and took up their weapons, and three times, Bobrok-Volinsky talked them down, reportedly using a whimsical turn of phrase: 'Wait a little, violent sons of Russia, the time will come when you'll feel better, because you'll have someone to play with!'

The *Expanded Chronicle Tale*, a colourful document that is distinctive on account of the heavy admixture of religious themes to its narrative, takes the traditional route of explaining the sudden reversal of fortunes for the Mongol-Tatars as being miraculous in origin. It recounts that God at that point 'looked on the princes of the Rus' with merciful eyes.' Suddenly angels swooped onto the battlefield to help them, and the princes Boris and Gleb – sainted sons of Prince Vladimir of Kiev, who had brought Christianity to Russia in the 8th century AD – led a regiment of heavenly warriors onto the field. As arrows of fire rained down upon them, 'the godless Tatars fell, overcome by their fear of God, and from the weapons of the Christians.' The truth may be less dramatic, but speaks more for Dmitry's planning and Russian fighting spirit.

Once Mamai's last forces were fully committed, and their flank exposed, then Bobrok-Volinsky unleashed Prince Vladimir and his eager regiment. They swept from the wood in a perfectly timed attack that pitted first-rank heavy cavalry desperate to avenge their comrades and led by one of the most respected fighting commanders in Russia against a makeshift force cobbled together from the leavings of a half-dozen detachments, many of which were already exhausted from previous fighting. This force may also have been under the command of Bulak Khan, nominal lord of Sarai, but in practice Mamai's captive and catspaw. His dreams of winning for himself the glory and respect worthy of a khan proved empty, as the Russians crashed into his formation. Bulak Khan fell on the field, surrounded by the bodies of his brief command. As the Tatars later mourned, 'the Rus' again outwitted us: we fought the younger ones, but the best still remained.' In other words, they tired themselves in battle against less experienced troops, while their enemy's best of the best had been kept fresh until the eleventh hour.

The fight was vicious but brief, and as the Ambush Regiment drove the survivors of Mamai's last gamble into the flanks of the Golden Horde units already locked in combat with the remnants of the Main Regiment,

This is a *lubok*, or cheap, popular print, of the kind used to decorate the walls of homes and shops of 19th-century Russia. They typically showed historical or religious scenes, and this tableau of Kulikovo is hardly a faithful representation but does show the Ambush Regiment in the woods to the top, ready to fall on Mamai's forces advancing from the right. (Public domain)

this disrupted them and heartened the Russians. Furthermore, the wind had changed, and, rather than blowing dust into the eyes of the Russians, it was now at their back. Suddenly, momentum swung away from the Tatars, and the Russians, reinvigorated, began pushing the invaders back across the battlefield. Unable to regroup, unsure of the scale of this new threat, Mamai's army wavered, then broke.

THE ROUT

'Swords were beating on the helmets of the infidels. The pagans were protecting their bodies with their hands. Then they began to retreat. Banners flapping, retreating from the Grand Prince, the pagans fled. The sons of Russia took the field, yelling, their helmets gleaming gold.'

The *Zadonshchina*

From his vantage point on Red Hill, Mamai must have watched with horrified dismay as what had looked to be imminent triumph suddenly turned into bloody disaster, with the breaking of his right flank under the hooves of the Ambush Regiment. To quote, appropriately enough, from *The Tale of the Rout of Mamai*, 'seeing new warriors gallop forth, who fell on their foe like savage beasts preying on a flock of sheep, he said to his own: "Let us flee, for we cannot wait to see if things get better, but at least we can save our heads!"' while 'many chased after them, they could not catch them, because their horses were tired, and Mamai's horses were fresh, and he left the chase behind him.'

So Mamai fled on a fast horse, with a relative handful of guards and retainers, thanks not only to his mount's fleetness of foot, but also the dogged persistence of those Genoese mercenaries who had been stationed at the Red Hill. They died almost to a man, but their last stand bought their employer the time to flee (a sacrifice he soon would have cause to regret). Many, perhaps even most, of his men would not be so fortunate.

In the words of the *Short Chronicle Tale*, 'God helped Grand Prince Dmitry Ivanovich, and Mamai's pagan troops ran away, and ours went after them, beating and cutting them down mercilessly.' As panic spread amongst the Golden Horde's forces, they scattered and fled, channelled by the battlefield back to the river Mecha, another tributary of the Don. If the battle had already been bloody enough, then, as usual in such fights, the rout was even bloodier. The Mecha was not especially wide, but fast flowing, and, in their desperation, riders fought riders, infantry were trampled underwater, and the failure of many horse nomads to learn how to swim spelled their doom. When they reached the Mecha, many of the Mongol-Tatars drowned, and many more were cut down by Russian arrows and blades. In the words of the *Sofia First Chronicle*, 'the River Don's waters were mixed with blood, heads of Tatars rolled like stones, pagan bodies fell like oaks.'

The Russian chronicles inevitably exaggerate the casualties even more enthusiastically than the original armies, with hundreds of thousands being cited (253,000 in the spuriously precise count of the *Zadonshchina*), or eight out of every nine invaders. Such a ratio is almost as implausible as the overall tallies, but either way it is clear that thousands of the invaders died, the army was broken, and, perhaps most crucially, the Russians also captured their

CHARGE OF THE AMBUSH REGIMENT (PP. 74–75)

This depicts the crucial moment in the battle, when the Ambush Regiment charges from the trees and into the flank of the Golden Horde forces that were moving to encircle the embattled Russian army. A Mongol infantry captain in lamellar armour (1) tries to issue commands to the horrified Armenian archers beside him (2), but there is simply no time. Prince Vladimir Andreyevich of Serpukhov (3), in the fore, wears heavy armour, including the distinctive Russian rimmed helmet, while his bannerman (4) is in opulent but more dated armour with decorations reminiscent of Scythian motifs, and bears the heart-shaped shield occasionally used by Russian noble cavalry.

baggage train and herds. This not only netted fortunes in plunder, it ended any prospect of a renewed advance before winter set in, even if the Mamai could have found the necessary troops.

Jogaila's Lithuanians, who by this time were only 35–40km (20–25 miles) away, turned back on hearing news of the defeat, to begin the long march home. In the *Chronik des Landes Prüssen*, Prussian priest Johann von Posilge claimed that the Russians then ran into them, while leaving the battle and the Lithuanians 'killed many of the Russians and took from them a large amount of booty that they took from the Tatars.' However, this seems unlikely as the only corroboration comes from other German sources that probably simply copied Posilge, and the chronology and routes simply do not match. Instead, as he was passing back through lands whose loyalties to him were questionable – the Lithuanian-controlled city of Polotsk had rebelled in 1378 and would again in 1381 – it is more likely he dawdled a little to assert his authority over these buffer territories, killing some Rus' and taking some plunder in the process. As for Prince Oleg of Ryazan, with nowhere else to go and no real alternative, he formally capitulated to Dmitry, although in practice it appears that he was able to withdraw to his city and await the consequences of his equivocation.

While the Russians held the field, though, they had paid a high and bitter price. At first it was feared that the real Dmitry had also perished in the close-quarters fighting before the ambush was sprung. Later accounts say that two soldiers from Kostroma found him after the battle, lying unconscious, surrounded by enemy dead. This is likely to be poetic licence, but more credible is the claim that his armour was battered and dented, suggesting

This 19th-century etching by Boris Chorikov includes some inaccurate clichés about Russian armour of the time, such as the vertical ridge running up the nose guard to the top on the helmets, but also accurately shows the large round medallion knights such as Dmitry often wore, as both protection and display. (Public domain)

This manuscript depiction of the Russian victory in the battle of the Vozha River in 1376 graphically shows fleeing Mongol-Tatars drowning in the river, a fate that would also befall many after Kulikovo. (Public domain)

both that – unusually for the time – he wore plate armour, but also that he had continued to be in the thick of the fighting. He had survived, and with him his coalition.

But the butcher's bill was a heavy one. Overall, the Russians had lost a third of their total number, perhaps even more. The *Zadonshchina* says that 'the corpses of Christians lay like stacks of haystacks, near the banks of the Great Don, and the Don River flowed with blood for three days.' The army would remain at Kulikovo for fully seven more days, gathering the dead from the field and burying them in communal graves (and presumably also living off the pickings of Mamai's captured baggage train). The prominent role of the boyar cavalry and the heroic tradition of leading from the front also ensured a gory tally of fallen aristocrats. Again to quote the *Zadonshchina*, according to a count by a Moscow boyar, Mikhail Alexandrovich, the fallen included 'forty boyars of Moscow, twelve princes of Belozersk, thirty Novgorod *posadniks* [militia commanders], twenty boyars of Kolomna, forty boyars of Serpukhov, thirty Lithuanian knights, twenty boyars of Pereyaslavl, twenty-five boyars of Kostroma, thirty-five boyars of Vladimir, fifty boyars of Suzdal, forty boyars of Murom, seventy boyars of Ryazan, thirty-four boyars of Rostov, twenty-three boyars of Dmitrovsk, sixty boyars from Mozhaisk, thirty boyars of Zvenigorodsk and fifteen boyars from Uglich.'

As ever, the specific detail can be questioned, not least as it seems to leave some detachments unscathed, and more generally the *Zadonshchina* needs to be treated with caution on casualties overall. The general picture is accurate in terms of the broad spread of the casualties, though. There are claims of losses in the tens of thousands, but Russian archaeologist Anatoly Kirpichnikov has produced a sober estimate that the Russians lost perhaps 800 boyars and 5,000–8,000 other soldiers. This was a victory, to be sure, but a victory bought with the blood of a significant proportion of the Russian principalities' feudal warrior-aristocracy, and it would leave them vulnerable – as Moscow would discover in 1382.

AFTERMATH

'And Prince Dmitry returned with a great victory, like Moses won against Amalek. And there was peace in the Russian land. And his enemies had been put to shame. Other nations, hearing about his God-given victories over his foes, all recognized his strength. The schismatics and rebels of his kingdom all perished.'

The *Story of the Life and Death of Grand Prince Dmitry Ivanovich*

Of course not everyone did live happily ever after, whatever the *Story of the Life and Death of Grand Prince Dmitry Ivanovich* might want to suggest. Nor was this a completely transformative moment, as later commentators have wanted to claim. The nationalist Russian historian Lev Gumilyov, for instance, wrote that 'men of Suzdal, of Vladimir, of Rostov, of Pskov, went to fight on Kulikovo Field as representatives of their principalities, but they returned from there Russians.' This is a fine piece of rhetoric but questionable history. First of all, the so-called 'Mongol Yoke' was relatively light; after the initial shock of the invasion, the Mongols proved relatively enlightened, even supportive overlords, as long as the tribute flowed. They may have been foreigners, but this was a term with little meaning in those days before clear borders and national identities, and much of the worst exploitation of the time was carried out by Russians preying on other Russians. Futhermore, this battle did not completely reshape the politics of the Rus' and certainly did not unify them, and did not mean that they would no longer have to pay the Golden Horde its tribute under threat of fire and sack. But at the same time, nor was it irrelevant. Dmitry himself was certainly eager to use it to the greatest advantage, and in the process arguably did accelerate the unification of the Rus' under Moscow and their emancipation from foreign rule.

This dramatic modern statue of Dmitry in Moscow, finally unveiled in 2013, represents an idealized version of the man and his history, with the inscription on the base proclaiming him 'liberator of Russia'. (© Mark Galeotti)

This 1,000-rouble Russian stamp from their 1995 'Great Princes' series shows Dmitry Donskoy flanked by images representing his roles as both city-builder and warleader. (Public domain)

DONSKOY TRIUMPHANT

'The brave knights, having tested their weapons enough upon the filthy Tatars, gathered from all directions to the trumpet's sound. They walked cheerfully, rejoicing, singing songs: they sang to the Mother of God, others sang to the martyrs, others sang psalms, but all sang Christian songs. Every warrior came, joyously, at the sound of the trumpet.'

The Tale of the Rout of Mamai

For the moment, Dmitry's victory meant peace. For him, his princes and his soldiers, it also meant the riches of plunder. The *Zadonshchina* makes no bones about this: 'The sons of Russia pillaged the Tatars of cloths and silks, weapons and horses, oxen and camels, wines and sugars, jewellery and velvets, and they carried the wealth of the Tatars to their wives. Tatar gold jingled in the hands of Russian woman.' Perhaps no wonder that 'Joy and happiness spread across the Russian land.' This meant more than just trinkets for the survivors' families. As soldiers returned home with inflated tales of heroism and miracles on the battlefield, and gold and silver in their pockets, they also bore the first versions of the legend of 'Dmitry Donskoy', the victor of the Don. (This title was also given to Prince Vladimir Andreyevich of Serpukhov, but was much less used after he fell out with Dmitry over the succession, in 1389.)

Along with his reputation, the Grand Prince also left Kulikovo with wagonloads of loot: money to fortify Moscow, reward loyal retainers, and buy new ones. He had taken with him on campaign ten merchants from Surozh in the Crimea (also known as Surak or, to the Italians, Soldaia), not just as sutlers and victuallers to supply the army as needed, but also as both sources of intelligence – for Crimea was held by the Golden Horde – and witnesses to his victory. By choosing outsiders, he presumably hoped they would be more credible amongst his friends and foes alike, again demonstrating his deft political skills. He moved quickly to parlay victory into greater authority among the Rus'. Governors for Muscovite vassal cities were announced to replace those who had fallen in battle. According to some accounts, Oleg of Ryazan, despite the equivocal nature of his support for Mamai, was forced to flee his city (it had not helped that some of his boyars, albeit without his permission, robbed wagons of loot on the way back from

Grand Prince Dmitry's official seal shows St George on one side, as patron saint of Moscow, and his title on the other. (Public domain)

Kulikovo) and a Muscovite voivode installed in his place. Others, though, assert that he was ruling the city still – or again – in 1382, so this is uncertain. Novgorod was encouraged retrospectively to applaud Moscow's leadership and victory, and its pragmatic willingness to do so helps explain the later myth that the only reason it did not participate in the battle was that it heard about it too late.

Dmitry, needless to say, wanted to have his cake, and eat it too. On the one hand, he presented himself as the foremost prince of the Rus', protecting its lands, cities and people from a Mongol punitive expedition and shattering an invading army. At the same time, he knew that Kulikovo had not upturned the political order, and that even many Rus' princes would hesitate before aligning themselves with an enemy of the Golden Horde. Interestingly enough, many of the contemporary accounts of the battle presented Dmitry not as a rebel, but a restorer of legitimate authority. Mamai was described as being a usurper of Sarai, a rebel against the righteous khans, and thus defying him was no more than being a good subject. This would not be enough to avert the inevitable revenge of the Golden Horde, though.

The ruins of the Genoese fortress at Caffa, now Feodosia, where Mamai finally met his end. (© Janmad)

MAMAI'S DOWNFALL

'But this time you, Tsar Mamai, came to the Russian land with a large army, with nine hordes and seventy princes, and yet you ran away to the sea, and with only eight soldiers. And you have no one to keep you company through the winter on the steppe.'

The *Zadonshchina*

After the battle, Mamai turned back eastwards and raised a new army, albeit of much less impressive numbers, to try and eject Tokhtamysh from Sarai. He was no more successful at this, his army being shattered at Kalka River in late 1380 or early 1381, not least because of massive defections to his enemy's camp. This defeat was, ironically, close to the spot where another western army had been broken by an eastern one – in that case Russians by Mongols – 150 years earlier. It was the end of his political career, his supporters abandoning him and his political – and economic – credit tapped out.

He was forced to flee to the Genoese port of Caffa in the Crimea (now known as Feodosia). According to one Russian chronicle, he took with him only eight guards but 'uncounted wealth, with much gold and silver, gems and pearls.' Whether he was hoping to hire enough mercenaries to retake Sarai or, more likely, was just fleeing with all the loot he could grab, he discovered that these were tough times. No one, it seems, loves a loser –

Tokhtamysh's Punitive Campaign, 1382

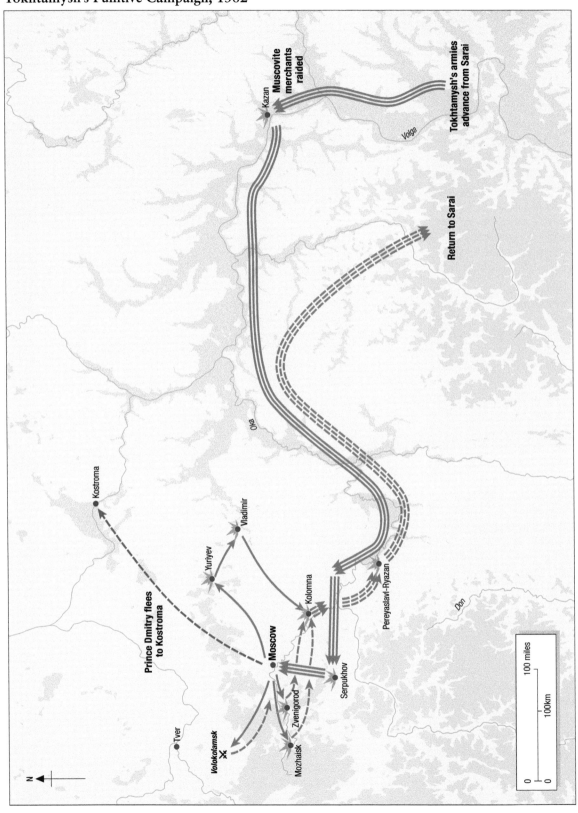

especially one who let hundreds of his countrymen die in vain while he fled, as Mamai had at Kulikovo.

According to the *Zadonshchina*, 'the infidel Mamai fled with his retainers like a grey wolf and ran to the city of Caffa on the sea. And the Italians asked him: "What's the matter, infidel Mamai, why did you dare invade the Russian lands?"' The Genoese promptly detained, and then executed him. Rather than simply a naked bid to steal his fortune, or take revenge for his cavalier treatment of the last soldiers he had hired from them, this was likely also to have been a cunning political move. Shortly thereafter, Tokhtamysh signed a treaty with the Genoese recognizing the autonomy of Caffa and granting them considerable trade rights. By ridding him of an irksome rival, the Genoese had earned themselves very generous terms indeed.

The Golden Horde's power was reaffirmed by Tokhtamysh with his seizure of Moscow in 1382. Apollinary Vasnetsov's *The Defence of Moscow from Khan Tokhtamysh* (1918) shows the muster of the city's defenders, many militia, before the ill-judged decision to open the gates when Tokhtamysh offered parley. (Public domain)

MOSCOW BURNS...

'There was a certain omen for many nights, a sign in the sky in the east before the early dawn: a particular star, as if tailed and like a spear, sometimes in the evening sun, sometimes in the morning; and many times this had happened before. This sign foreshadowed the evil coming of Tokhtamysh to the Russian land and the harrowing invasion of Christendom by the pagan Tatars.'

The *Tale of Tokhtamysh*

One could argue that the true victor of Kulikovo was Tokhtamysh. His rival, Mamai, was humbled and soon killed, while the flower of Russian military aristocracy was left dead on the field. The *Zadonshchina* may have claimed that 'The Tatar lands groaned with grief upon grief, filled with grief: the desire of its kings and princes to go to the Russian land disappeared', but Tokhtamysh was determined to demonstrate at once that the Russians still needed to pay tribute and that he was no Mamai. In 1382, when the princes of the Rus' politely declined to come to Sarai personally to swear their allegiance (no doubt fearing they would be taken hostage or made an example of), he gathered at least 30,000 men and launched a punitive expedition aimed squarely at Moscow. Dmitry's admirers may have sought to present him as an enemy of Mamai the usurper, not the Golden Horde as a whole, but Tokhtamysh was a man who appears to have lacked patience with such subtleties.

It says much about both the weakened state of Russia's principalities after the Pyrrhic victory of Kulikovo, and the continued divisions between them, that Dmitry could muster few allies to resist this renewed threat. In the words of the *Tale of Tokhtamysh*, 'there was disagreement among the princes, and they did not want to help each other, nor did they want to help each brother's brother.' Indeed, one-eyed Dmitry Konstantinovich

'And they faced a fourfold destruction: the first, by the sword, second by the fire, the third by the water, and the fourth by all of them.' A depiction of the sack of Moscow by Tokhtamysh in 1382, as desperate civilians try to flee the flames and the swords of the Mongol-Tatar troops in the background. (Public domain)

of Suzdal had no qualms about actively joining with Tokhtamysh's forces in humbling his old rival, Dmitry of Moscow. Two of his sons, Vasily and Semyon, are reported as having proved crucial in delivering the city to the Mongol-Tatar besiegers.

Dmitry and his family had already fled north-east to Kostroma, before Tokhtamysh's army arrived, and the city was encircled. Yet after a moment of panic, in which 'like sheep without a shepherd, the townspeople became agitated and raged like drunks,' the Muscovites rallied. They reminded themselves, in the words of the *Tale of Tokhtamysh*, that they were in 'such a strong city: its walls are stone and the gate is iron,' and assembled their forces, arming a militia and gathering supplies. For three days and nights of siege, Moscow held behind the new brick and stone walls Dmitry had built, their defence including the first registered use of firearms in a Russian conflict.

Eventually, the city fell to subterfuge as Tokhtamysh, supported by the princes of Suzdal, persuaded the defenders to open their gates, saying that his quarrel was with Dmitry and not the people of Moscow 'because you are innocent and do not deserve death... The king does not demand anything else from you, just go out to meet him with honours and gifts, as he wishes to see this city, and enter it, and visit it, and he will give you peace and love, and you open the gate of the city for him.'

Unsurprisingly, it was a ruse, and the attackers stormed in through the open gates, scaled the undefended walls, and massacred those who stood before them. The city was sacked and burned; one chronicler lamented afterwards, 'nothing could be seen but smoking ruins and bare earth and heaps of corpses, and the holy churches stood ravaged, as if orphaned, as if widowed.' This was something of an exaggeration, though, and, despite the deaths and enslavement of probably tens of thousands of its inhabitants, Moscow – which, like all Russian cities, had sadly become used to occasional sackings – was quickly rebuilt.

...BUT MOSCOW ALSO TRIUMPHS

> 'And the princes of Russia and his nobles answered [Dmitry]: Sir, our Russian Tsar! We promised to serve you, to give our lives for you, and now we will shed our blood for you, and with our blood we will take the second baptism.'
>
> The *Story of the Life and Death of Grand Prince Dmitry Ivanovich*

Although other cities also suffered, Tokhtamysh clearly set out to humble and weaken Moscow, as he continued to attack a series of other Muscovite holdings. Vladimir and Zvenigorod, Mozhaisk and Dmitrov, Pereyaslavl and Kolomna, the campaign picked off city after city and, in the coy words of the chronicle, 'a lot of evil was brought to Russia.' It continued:

How many were lost to that military invasion, how many cities they captured, how much gold, and silver, and treasure was taken, and how many goods, how many villages and towns were destroyed, and how many were burned, how many were swept away by the sword, how many were ended! And if I could count all the hardships, misfortunes, and losses, I do not dare to say, but I think that even a thousand thousand rubles is not equal to their number!

Eventually, though, Tokhtamysh returned to Sarai, and the political, military and economic realities of the time reasserted themselves. The ravaging of Moscow did not reverse the decline of the Golden Horde in the long term, nor the continuing ascendancy of Moscow under Dmitry's descendants. After all, it is striking that even with Moscow burning, Dmitry and the Ryurikids were powers among the Rus', with whom Tokhtamysh still had to deal. He sent his emissary, one Karach, to broker an agreement, which essentially allowed Moscow to return to the pre-Mamai status quo. That Dmitry had to reaffirm allegiance to the Golden Horde is less significant than that the Golden Horde – in the form of Tokhtamysh – had to give him that option, and to confirm him as Grand Prince of Vladimir in the process. For the rest of his short life (he died nine years after Kulikovo, according to some, as a result of injuries suffered in the battle), Dmitry could continue to expand his patrimony as freely as before.

Prince Oleg may have been damned as a traitor by the Muscovites at the time, but he is still regarded as one of the great rulers of the city at home, as shown by this modern statue in Ryazan's Cathedral Square. (© Nikita Zimin)

Indeed, poor Ryazan, which had also been sacked by Tokhtamysh (more on general principle than for any other reason) suffered the same fate again at the hands of the Muscovites after the Golden Horde's forces withdrew, and a voivode had definitely been assigned to govern the city in the Grand Prince's name by 1383. This was both belated punishment for backing Mamai and also to raise loot to help in the reconstruction of their own city. In 1385, though, Oleg of Ryazan was allowed to return to his principality, albeit only by pledging the same fealty to Dmitry as a 'little brother' to Moscow, as had previously been forced on Prince Mikhail of Tver.

For a century, until Mongol-Tatar forces were faced down by Grand Prince Ivan III at the Ugra River in 1480, Moscow and the other Russian cities still had, off and on, to pay tribute to the Golden Horde, and Moscow's princes were still among Sarai's most assiduous local agents. Over time, though, morally ambiguous reality would be replaced by dramatic and heroic legend. Kulikovo become central to the mythologies of a rising Russia, with the Ryurikids' early careers as Mongol enforcers, tax collectors, and administrators forgotten in the name of building a grand narrative of national resurgence and independence.

The *Story of the Life and Death of Grand Prince Dmitry Ivanovich* was written either shortly after his death in 1389, or early in the next century, and is a much more obvious piece of propaganda than more contemporary accounts. Already by then Dmitry was being lauded as 'a Russian tsar' – the term tsar, or emperor, was only really applied in the 16th century – such that as 'the glory of his name grew... the Russian land was flourishing like the promised land of Israel in the past.' Kulikovo thus becomes a central triumph, a defence of Russia and Christendom alike from a Mamai who is claimed to boast, 'I will conquer the Russian lands and destroy Christian churches and

A perfect illustration of the fusion of Church, history and politics is the Temple-Monument Named for the Holy Grand Prince Dmitry Donskoy in Nizhny Tagil. This modern church, consecrated in 2003 but explicitly built along medieval lines, was built in memory not so much of the prince, but the 'Dmitry Donskoy Tank Column', a formation funded by donations from believers and deployed in 1944 during World War II. It is sited next to the entrance to the Uralvagonzavod tank factory. (Creative Commons: Tara-Amingu)

The Mongols were conquerors, not administrators, and they relied on local princes and elders to assemble the tribute they demanded from their subject people. This painting, by Sergei Ivanov, shows a Mongol *baskak*, an official responsible for collecting that tribute and enforcing the census, being welcomed into a village. While he is in formal dress, note the armoured captain of his soldiers behind him, his face hidden behind a mail veil. (Public domain)

convert them to my faith, and make them bow to Mohammed... [I will] place my officials in all Russian cities and kill the Russian princes.' Unsurprisingly, supported by the united efforts of all Russia's princes (Ryazan, Novgorod and other holdouts are glossed over), as well as divine intervention, Dmitry triumphs and Russia is free – and Tokhtamysh's subsequent intervention and other tiresome facts are also neatly ignored. The scene is set for another six centuries of myth-making.

Yet the fact is that, even scrubbed clear of all the elaborations and exaggerations, Kulikovo was indeed a dramatic feat, a genuine, if costly victory. It was a political triumph, as Dmitry managed to bring together an unprecedented coalition of Russia's fractious and jealous princes. It was a military triumph, as the Russians not only weathered but broke an attack by a larger force of enemies, mainly made up of the fearsome Mongol-Tatar warriors who had once had the world at their feet. And it was a cultural triumph, creating a powerful image around which the still-nascent Russian identity could begin to cohere.

In his revised will and testament, written shortly before his death, Dmitry Donskoy held out the promise of a Russia free from what would later be called the 'Mongol Yoke', noting, 'if God brings about a change regarding the Horde [and] my children do not have to give Tatar tribute to the Horde, then the tribute that each of my sons collects in his patrimonial principality shall be his.' It would take another hundred years for the last vestiges of Mongol-Tatar domination to be lost, but thanks in part to Kulikovo, that day was coming.

THE BATTLEFIELD TODAY

'The Battle on Kulikovo Field did not end the era of the Tatar-Mongol yoke, but this battle proved to everyone that the mighty strength of Russia was like a powerful coil, capable of springing out and throwing back any opponent, and go on to win.'

Patriarch Kirill, 2010

A 1914 poster depicted Dmitry Donskoy in a bid to bolster patriotism amongst Russians at the start of World War I and persuade them to donate to victims of the war. This was not just a random historical choice, as Donskoy and Kulikovo were very much in the public imagination. That same year, popular Romantic artist Viktor Vasnetsov had finished his iconic painting of the clash between Peresvet and Chelubey. Just in 1908, Alexander Blok had published his poem 'On Kulikovo Field', lyrically recalling the battlefield, and before then, painter Valentin Serov had produced 'After the Battle of Kulikovo', evoking the victory and loss of the battle. In short, while Kulikovo may have been a 14th-century battle, it was still being appropriated and represented in the 20th century, just as it is today, as a clear sign of its significance to Russia's historical self-image.

THE INVISIBLE BATTLEFIELD

'The circumstances of this war have been so distorted by the rhetoric and the discrepancies of the chroniclers that it is very difficult to see the reality in these many variations and additions.'

19th-century historian Nikolai Artsybashev

Was there even a battle at Kulikovo? Modern Tatar historian Rustam Nabiyev has cast doubt on the idea that the battle took place. Instead, he argues, Dmitry and the other Russian princes actually took part in the battle in 1381 in which Mamai was trounced by Tokhtamysh. This frames the battle not as a blow for Russian nationhood, but an example of loyal subjects of the Golden Horde helping topple a usurper, and so it is perhaps surprising that many Russian historians have furiously denounced the very notion as 'Tatar chauvinism'.

That said, the fact of the battle seems hard ultimately to be denied. A rather more extensive historical controversy continues over the precise location of the site. Fought as it was, away from any settlements or even fixed

This poster from 1914, invoked Dmitry Donskoy's legend to encourage Russians to donate to a fund for victims of World War I. (Public domain)

landmarks – as the Don and its tributaries have meandered over time – the place where so many warriors fought and died was lost for centuries. It took an amateur archaeologist, the church official and poet Stepan Nechayev, first to locate the site, make some initial research digs, and even set up a small private museum with his finds. This created a groundswell of opinion that led to Tsar Alexander I's decision to approve the building of a monument at Red Hill.

Nonetheless, for years archaeologists and historians were baffled by the relative absence of finds, given that, as far as knowledge at the time went, this field had witnessed an epic battle between not tens, but hundreds of thousands of men. This also provided ammunition for those who doubted it was the right site, especially based on readings of the Bulgar chronicles. Many of these doubts have since been addressed, although it has to be said that in many ways the best argument is that none of the proposed alternative sites has revealed any more impressive archaeological evidence. First of all, and most obviously, the size of the armies was much smaller than the more extravagant chronicles suggested. Many of the Mongol-Tatar casualties, besides, were suffered not on Kulikovo field, but in the subsequent rout, their bodies scattered on the way to the Mecha or swept away by the river. There has indeed been a distinct series of finds precisely in a corridor from Kulikovo to the Mecha. Secondly, there was likely to have been extensive scavenging of the battlefield over the years, not least by the victors themselves. The account that the Russians spent a week collecting the dead suggests more than simply reverential treatment of the fallen. Thirdly, a combination of agricultural practices and soil chemistry combined in a destructive way. The thick black earth is notoriously corrosive of bodies and even metal, and the cheap ammonium nitrate fertilizer favoured in Soviet times also had a tendency to break down metal. However, when more advanced technologies such as ground-penetrating radar could be used, a series of mass burial pits were located, as well as a greater range of metal debris presumed to be from the battle.

KULIKOVO TODAY

'In the military history of Russia there are three Great Russian battlefields, the three most important battles took place on them. They are the Kulikovo Field, the Prokhorovskoye Field and the Borodino Field.'

Official website of the Kulikovo Field State Museum of Military History

Today, there is little that is truly authentic about Kulikovo, but a determined attempt to restore it – for reasons of both tourism and national pride – has made some progress ever since the establishment of the Kulikovo Field State Museum of Military History and Natural Reserve in 1996. A four-hour drive from Moscow (it is not especially conveniently sited for other means of transport), the site increasingly attracts tourists, as well as hosting an annual re-enactment festival attended by tens of thousands of visitors and enthusiasts.

The site itself is some 5km (3 miles) from the more modern village of Monastyrshchino. In the late 17th century, a simple wooden church was built here to remember the dead, though, even by then, the exact location of the battle and the mass graves had become uncertain. After all, the rivers meandered over the centuries, and the Smolka and Nizhny Dubik have become shallower and slower than they were in the 14th century. Generations of agricultural production and improvement ploughed up the land, especially during the Soviet era, with its infatuation with mechanized farming, and stripped away the forests that played such a crucial role in the battle.

In due course, though, paleobotanical researchers have helped identify the boundaries of the old forests and a process of replanting is under way, especially of the Wood of Green Oaks, where the Ambush Regiment laid its trap (marked with a large white cross laid out on the turf). With the territory

Vasily Nikitich Tatishchev, the 18th-century historian, geographer and statesman, who not only founded the cities of Stavropol (now Tolyatti), Yekaterinburg and Perm, but did much to popularize the medieval chronicles which remain the key sources for the battle of Kulikovo. (Public domain)

Re-enactors in a mix of lamellar and scale armour, before a bell and banners. Note the representation of a mounted St George slaying a dragon on the right-hand flag, the symbol of Moscow. (© Petr Shelomovskiy)

This panoramic shot of the battlefield museum clearly shows both the way it is sunk into Kulikovo Field and also the use of spears to mark the trail. (© Avsolov)

now designated a State Museum-Preserve, farmland has been returned to the wild, and one can again see the grassy steppe on which so much blood was shed.

There are three main parts to the Kulikovo Field State Museum of Military History and Natural Reserve: the Kulikovo Field museum, the Monastyrshchino Museum-Memorial Complex and the Red Hill Memorial. The battlefield museum itself is an impressive, modern structure, opened only in 2016. It was described by *Architectural Review* as 'carved out of the battlefield itself... a collision of high-tech and tradition' and it is hard to disagree. Built in and within a mound consciously echoing the funeral mounds of the early Slavs (and approximately as tall as the Red Hill), it takes visitors through the prelude and the battle, before leading them by paths marked by spears of light driven into the ground to an observation deck from which they can look out across the field itself. Bells ring every day to mark the time the fighting started and ended.

The austere 28m-high (90ft) iron monument at Kulikovo, erected in 1850. (© Arssenev)

The Monastyrshchino complex comprises the Museum of the Battle of Kulikovo, the temple of Nativity of the Virgin Mary, a monument to Dmitry Donskoy, and the Unity and Memory Alley, commemorating cities which contributed detachments to the Russian army and heroes from them. A new museum replaced the old one in 2000, and it is a large and impressive one, with halls showcasing life at the time of the battle in both Russia and the Golden Horde, as well as weapons and armour, and a diorama of the battle. It is also used for events such as the regular *Marsh-brosok* regional school and university student games, described as 'a real test for future defenders of the Fatherland', in which teams compete in a series of events, from rifle shooting and metal detecting, to an obstacle course, 10km (6 miles) quick march and even a Russian history quiz.

Since 1850, on Red Hill, where Mamai had established his command post, there has stood a column honouring Dmitry Donskoy, a 28m (90ft) obelisk of cast iron, topped with a golden onion dome and cross. Originally, huts were built alongside the monument where retired soldiers, hired to guard it, lived (as a reward for good service). Over time, they

became the first guides to the battlefield, as it began to become a destination for historical pilgrimage in the latter half of the 19th century. The huts fell into disrepair in the 20th century, but in recent years they have been restored, to provide offices for museum staff.

During World War I, inspired by the burst of desperate patriotism that characterized 1914, the Orthodox Church decided to build the Temple-Monument in the name of St Sergius of Radonezh, right next to the obelisk. It was completed on the eve of the Bolshevik revolution of 1917. Its architect, Alexander Shchusev – who would later design the mausoleum for Lenin that still stands on Red Square – had plans to make this part of a whole Red Hill museum complex. However, as the church fell into disfavour and Soviet Russia was wracked by Civil War and transformed by reconstruction, this idea fell by the wayside. Kulikovo became cultivated collective farmland and it was only in the 1960s that there began to be renewed interest in the site. In 1965, a branch of Tula Region Local History Museum opened here, but this initially comprised a single employee, one Klavdia Alekseyeva, who lived and worked in a small cottage. Only in 1980 was a proper museum opened in the temple-monument. In 2010 the temple-monument was returned to the Orthodox Church, and it is no longer a museum but a restored church.

As Kulikovo is both restored and also promoted as the site of a pivotal moment in Russian nationhood, it is becoming more visitor friendly, such as with this representational map of the battlefield. (© Quagdu)

A SHRINE TO RUSSIA

'We celebrate him, on the first military field of Russia, because if there had been no Sergius [of Radonezh], there would have been no battle. And maybe no Russia.'

Patriarch Kirill

Even if Sergius of Radonezh had no real role in the battle, Patriarch Kirill – speaking in 2014 next to Prime Minister Dmitry Medvedev at the anniversary of the battle – was eager to claim credit for the Orthodox Church. This is hardly surprising, because history (or at least a convenient version of it) has become closely connected with Vladimir Putin's nation-building project and

also a revival of public interest, after the leaden ideological correctness of Soviet scholarship. This is especially visible in the annual Kulikovo Field International Military History Festival, that attracts not just hundreds of re-enactors from across Russia and abroad, but also almost as many spectators across its four days as actual participants in the original battle. It is the oldest and largest re-enactment festival in Russia, and also inevitably the beneficiary of the state's growing interest in fostering patriotic sentiment by selective cherry-picking of Russian history. In 2012, President Vladimir Putin – known to be a keen reader of history – set up the Russian Military-Historical Society, which now co-funds this and almost two dozen other such festivals. (Unexpectedly, the re-enactment is held around 21 September, because of the effect of Russia's switch from the Julian to the Gregorian calendars in 1918.)

This assiduous rediscovery (and sometimes careful redefinition) of past military glories is not purely a political gambit by a government eager to affirm Russia's status as a great power. It also reflects the return of history after the collapse of the Soviet Union at the end of 1991, with all that regime's efforts to re-invest its past, and the rediscovery of the Orthodox faith. In this respect, the story of Dmitry Donskoy and Kulikovo conveniently brings together the rise of Muscovy, the defence of the Motherland against a seemingly unbeatable foe, and also the power of Russian Orthodoxy. According to an official school textbook

Russian monasteries of the middle ages were as much fortified strongholds as religious centres. This monastery, founded in in 1591 to commemorate the defeat of the Crimean Khan Kazy-Girey, was built on the site of one of Sergius of Radonezh's churches to draw a direct link with the battle of Kulikovo. Conveniently enough, the position also allowed it to command Moscow's southern approaches. (© Mark Galeotti)

adopted in 2013, this was when 'the light of freedom began to dawn' as 'victory on the field of Kulikovo roused the national awareness of the Russian people.'

Dmitry became a saint of the Russian Orthodox faith in 1988. He is now commemorated across the country, in a revival of those tsarist-era traditions which had seen the Donskoy Monastery in Moscow founded in 1591 as both a religious retreat and defensive bastion for the city, for example, and Dmitry figure prominently in the 'Millennium of Russia' statue erected in Novgorod in 1862 to celebrate the founding fathers of the nation. Now, there are also impressive statues of him in Kolomna (2007) and Moscow (2014).

Nor is he remembered only through memorials. As of writing, the TK-208 *Dmitry Donskoy* is the largest submarine in active service in the world, a nuclear ballistic missile boat of the Project 941 Akula class (known by the NATO reporting name Typhoon) operating within Russia's Northern Fleet and capable of launching 20 nuclear missiles. One of the MiG-29 fighters based in Armenia in 2014 was emblazoned with an image of St Dmitry. The 51st Guards Airborne Regiment of the 106th Air Assault Division is named after Dmitry Donskoy. The 33rd Special Purpose Detachment of the Interior Troops, since 2016 incorporated into the new National Guard, is called 'Peresvet' after Donskoy's warrior-monk champion. In short, today's Russia very much considers itself the heir to the victory of Kulikovo and will continue to mobilize it to assert its determination to defend itself and its status as a great military power.

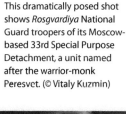

This dramatically posed shot shows *Rosgvardiya* National Guard troopers of its Moscow-based 33rd Special Purpose Detachment, a unit named after the warrior-monk Peresvet. (© Vitaly Kuzmin)

BIBLIOGRAPHY

Amel'kin, Andrei O. & Seleznev, Yurii, V., *Kulikovskaia bitva v svidetel'stvakh sovremennikov i pamiati potomkov* ('The Battle of Kulikovo in Contemporary Accounts and the Memories of Posterity'), Kvadriga, Moscow (2011)

Beskrovnyi, Lyobimir G. et al. (eds), *Kulikovskaya bitva: Sbornik statei* ('The Battle of Kulikovo: a collection of articles'), Nauka, Moscow (1980)

Blok, Alexander (trans. Robin Kemball), 'On the Field of Kulikovo' in *Russian Review* 13.1 (1954), pp.33–37

Buganov, Victor Ivanovich, *Kulikovskaia Bitva* ('The Battle of Kulikovo'), Pedagogica, Moscow (1985)

Carleton, Gregory, *Russia: the Story of War*, Harvard University Press, Boston (2017)

Carpini, Giovanni Di Piano, *The Story of the Mongols whom we call the Tatars*, Branden, Boston (1996)

Chambers, James, *The Devil's Horsemen. The Mongol Invasion of Europe*, Castle, Edison NJ (2003)

Crummey, Robert, *The Formation of Muscovy, 1304–1613*, Longman, Harlow (1987)

De Hartog, Leo, *Russia and the Mongol Yoke: The History of the Russian Principalities and the Golden Horde, 1221–1502*, British Academic Press, London (1996)

Dvurechenskii, O.V., et al, *Relikvii Donskogo poboishcha. Nakhodki na Kulikovom pole* ('Relics of the Battle of the Don. Finds from Kulikovo Field'), Kvadriga, Moscow (2008)

Garzeniti, Marcello, 'Le origini medievali della "santa Russia". La commemorazione della battaglia di Kulikovo (1380) nella "Narrazione del massacro di Mamaj" ('The Medieval Origins of "Holy Russia". The commemoration of the battle of Kulikovo (1380) in the "Tale of the Rout of Mamai") in *Reti Medievali Rivista* 17.1 (2016), pp.35–70

Gorelik, Mikhail, *Armii Mongolo-Tatar X–XIV vv* ('The Mongol-Tatar Armies of the 10th–14th Centuries'), Vostochnyi gorizont, Moscow (2002)

Halperin, Charles J., 'The Ideology of Silence: Prejudice and Pragmatism on the Medieval Religious Frontier' in *Comparative Studies in Society and History*, 26.3 (1984), pp.442–466

Halperin, Charles J., *The Tatar Yoke*, Slavica, Columbus (1986)

Halperin, Charles J., 'The Battle of Kulikovo Field (1380) in history and historical memory' in *Kritika* 14.4 (2013), pp.853–864

Halperin, Charles J., 'A Tatar interpretation of the battle of Kulikovo Field, 1380: Rustam Nabiev' in *Nationalities Papers*, 44.1 (2016), pp.4–19

Heath, Ian, *Armies of the Middle Ages Vol. 2: The Ottoman Empire, Eastern Europe and the Near East, 1300–1500*, Flexprint, Sussex (1984)

Kaiser, Daniel & Marker, Gary (eds), *Reinterpreting Russian History. Readings, 860–1860s*, OUP, Oxford (1994)

Kargalov, Vadim V., *Kulikovskaya bitva* ('The Battle of Kulikovo'), Voenizdat, Moscow (1980)

Kirpichnikov, A.N., *Voennoe delo na Rusi v XIII–XV vv* ('Military Affairs in Russia in the 13th–15th Centuries'), Lenizdat, Leningrad (1976)

Kotker, Norman, 'Kulikovo Field' in *Military History Quarterly* 6.1 (1993), pp.20–31

Lebedev, E.N., *Zadonshchina*, Sovremennik, Moscow (1980)

Martin, Janet, *Medieval Russia 980–1584*, Cambridge University Press, Cambridge (1996)

Nicolle, David, *Armies of Medieval Russia 750–1250*, Osprey Publishing, Oxford (1999)

Nicolle, David & Shpakovsky, Viacheslav, *Kalka River 1223*, Osprey Publishing, Oxford (2001)

Nossov, Konstantin, *Medieval Russian Fortresses AD 862–1480*, Osprey Publishing, Oxford (2007)

Oliphant, Roland, 'The Russian reenactors wearing armour to "feel free"' in *Sunday Telegraph*, 1 November 2015

Parppei, Kati, *The Battle of Kulikovo Refought. 'The First National Feat'*, Brill, Leiden (2017)

Rostovtsev, Evgeny, & Sosnitsky, Dmitry, '"The Kulikovo Captivity": The Image of Dmitry Donskoy in National Historical Memory' in *Quaestio Rossica* 5.4 (2017), pp.1149–1163

Rybakov, Boris, *Kievskaya Rus'* ('Kievan Rus')', Molodaya Gvardiya, Moscow (1984)

Shcherbakov, A. & Dzys', I., *Kulikovskaya bitva, 1380* ('The Battle of Kulikovo, 1380'), Exprint, Moscow (2001)

Shlyakhtorov, Alexei, *Kak Zolotaya Orda ozolotila Rus'. Mify i pravda o 'tataro-mongol'skom ige'* ('How the Golden Horde Gilded Russia. Myths and Truth about the "Tatar-Mongol yoke"'), Litres, Moscow (2017)

Shpakovsky, Viacheslav & Nicolle, David, *Medieval Russian Armies 1250–1500*, Osprey Publishing, Oxford (2002)

Shpakovsky, Viacheslav & Nicolle, David, *Armies of the Volga Bulgars & Khanate of Kazan*, Osprey Publishing, Oxford (2013)

Spinei, Victor & Bilavschi, George (eds), *Russian and Mongols: Slavs and the Steppe in Medieval and Early Modern Russia*, Editura Academiei Române, Bucharest (2007)

Suggs, William H., 'In search of the Bogatyri: The need for a new myth in the Soviet army' in *The Journal of Soviet Military Studies* 4.3 (1991), pp.506–512

Turnbull, Stephen, *The Mongols*, Osprey Publishing, Oxford (1980)

Zenkovsky, Serge (ed), *Medieval Russia's Epics, Chronicles and Tales, revised and enlarged version*, Meridian, New York (1974)

INDEX

Page number in **bold** refer to illustrations and their captions.